Moving Higher

Achieving Change in Nonprofit Organizations

Chukwuemeka Umeh

Printed in the United States of America

First Printing: 2017

10-digit ISBN: 1542748712
13-digit ISBN: 978-1542748711

Lois & Bryant LLC
Winchester, California. USA.
emmyumeh@yahoo.com

CONTENTS

PREFACE..V

CHAPTER 1 MOVING HIGHER 1

CHAPTER 2 PREPARING THE NEST FOR THE EGG......................9

CHAPTER 3 GETTING THE STAFF IN HIGH SPIRITS 29

CHAPTER 4 TURNING THE INVISIBLE INTO THE VISIBLE.......51

CHAPTER 5 USING THE ANTS' STRATEGY 65

CHAPTER 6 SHOWING EACH OTHER THE WAY 81

CHAPTER 7 EMPLOYING THE POWER OF SYNERGY.................95

REFERENCES 109

PREFACE

In my work with nonprofit organizations, I met several leaders who desperately wanted to implement changes in their organizations but failed even after they had put in what they thought were their best efforts. I have also seen the frustration of leaders whose efforts at change failed. An executive director of one of such organizations tried twice to implement change and failed. In frustration, he fired some key staff who he felt were instrumental in making the staff body resist the organizational change; but unfortunately, that still did not lead to the desired change in the organization. Furthermore, I recently came across three organizations that closed because their leaders did not succeed in making the changes they knew were necessary for the survival of their organizations. This difficulty in effecting change is the reason I am excited to share the experiences of resource-constrained nonprofit organizations that against all odds successfully implemented changes in their organizations. This book is born out of my experience studying the capacity development of 135 nonprofit organizations in two different countries over a period of three years. In "Moving Higher" I review six steps which I found in organizations that effectively utilized their limited resources to change and improve their organizational capacity.

This book would not have been possible without the help of several people. I want to thank Professors Malcolm Bryant, Jon Simon, Frank Feeley, Lois McCloskey, Nafisa Halim, and Taryn Vian for their great support. In addition, I will not fail to thank Ikechi and Stella Onyi, Davies Alozie, Kelvin Umeh, Chijioke

Okoro, Joseph Olunwa, and Folorunsho David for their support and inputs. I am also very appreciative of the loving support of my wife, Abigail.

Chukwuemeka Anthony Umeh

CHAPTER 1
MOVING HIGHER

Organizational change is a result of diligent planning and action by organizations that believe that they can change and persevere in the change process
-Chukwuemeka Umeh

O rganizations need to continuously change, adapt, and improve in order to be competitive and survive in a fast changing world. However, change does not usually happen arbitrarily. It requires a change champion who understands that though change is needed, it cannot be a one-man show. It takes a change champion who appreciates the great resources in other members of staff, engages them in deciding the scope and the process of change, motivates them to take ownership of the change, and provides conditions for collaboration and learning within the organization and between the organization and other organizations. This book outlines the factors that helped change champions to effectively implement change in different non-governmental organizations in Ethiopia and Nigeria. These factors were findings from a three-year Boston University Center for Global Health and Development (CGHD) organizational development study in Ethiopia and Nigeria. In this first chapter, I will briefly explain the type of organizations we worked with, the way we assessed the change in their capacity, and the summary of our findings.

In 2012, Boston University's Center for Global Health and Development (CGHD) received a three-year grant to conduct a longitudinal prospective study of organizational development of non-governmental organizations (NGOs) working with orphans and vulnerable children (OVC) in Ethiopia. In 2015, the grant was extended for another one year in order to evaluate the organizational development of NGOs in Nigeria among other things. These were some of the objectives of our study:

1. To assess the capacity and the level of development of NGOs serving OVCs

2. To longitudinally examine changes in the capacity and the level of development of the NGOs

The NGOs involved in this study work with orphans and vulnerable children (OVCs); persons living with HIV (PLHIV); some key populations (men who have sex with men, transgender people, people who inject drugs, and sex workers); youths; and pregnant mothers. These NGOs engage in multiple service areas including education, health, economic strengthening, agriculture, water hygiene and sanitation, and cultural heritage preservation.

We partnered with three organizations in Ethiopia (Pact Ethiopia, Save the Children/US, and the Consortium for Christian Relief Development Associations) and two in Nigeria (Pact Nigeria and Association of OVC NGOs of Nigeria) that provide capacity building support and funding to NGOs. These partners introduced us to 44 NGOs in Ethiopia and 91 in Nigeria who became the cohort of organizations for the study. The study in Ethiopia was a three-year longitudinal prospective study while that of Nigeria was for six months. We assessed the baseline organizational capacities of the Ethiopian NGOs in 2012 and reassessed them in 2013 and 2014 to evaluate the changes in the organizations. In Nigeria, we assessed the baseline organizational capacities of the organizations in 2015 and reassessed in 2016.

The NGOs varied greatly in age, size, annual budget, and geographic location but all served child populations in urban and semi-urban Ethiopia and Nigeria. The average age of the NGOs in Ethiopia was 14 years and the organizations were based in five different regions of Ethiopia. The mean annual budget (as reported in the external audit report) in 2012 was $985,679. Sixteen organizations reported having unrestricted funds. The mean staff size was 89 and ranged from 4 to 358. The average number of volunteers was 596. All the organizations had a board of directors, with a mean board membership of 8 (range 5 – 53). Females are under-represented in the boards with only 31% of the board members being female. On average, the boards met seven times in the last one year prior to the first assessment of the organizations.

In Nigeria, the average age of the organizations was 13 years and the organizations were based in seven different states in Nigeria. The average number of staff in the organizations was 19 with a range of 3 to 39 and one organization having 562 staff. Fifty one percent of the staff were female. There was an average of 40 volunteers per organization and this ranged from 0 to 165, with one organization having 1151 volunteers. The mean budget for 2015 was $109,281. Thirty seven organizations reported having unrestricted funds. All but one of the organizations had a board of directors, with a mean board membership of 6.6 (range 4 – 19). Females are under-represented in the boards with only 15% of the board members being female. On average, the boards met twice in the last one year prior to the first assessment of the organizations.

Table 1: Characteristics of Organizations Involved in the Study

	Ethiopia	Nigeria
Number of organizations	44	91
Mean age of organizations (years)	14	13
Mean number of staff	89	19
Mean annual Budget	$985,679	$109,281

In order to measure organizational change, we constructed a new tool around existing organizational capacity assessment tools which responded to identified assessment tool weaknesses such as lack of objectivity, lack of rigor, lack of replicability, and high burden on NGO staff and resources. The resulting Measuring Organizational Development and Effectiveness tool (MODE) measures organizational capacity and change in capacity in 11 different domains:

- Mission and Values
- Leadership and Governance
- Strategic Planning

- Operational Planning
- Management of People
- Linkages and Communication
- Logistics Management
- Quality Management
- Management of Information
- Financial Management and Budgeting
- Financial Security and Fundraising

The MODE tool measures both types of change that occur in an organization receiving capacity-building intervention:

- ➢ Mechanical change – change in the processes, systems, and structures of the organization--such as, in human resources policy, financial management policy, office procedures, etc.
- ➢ Behavioral change – change in the way people in the organization do things. It is considered the more important of the two but the more difficult to accomplish.

So for example, we did not only assess if organizations have produced a strategic plan (mechanical change), but we also assessed if they are using the plan (behavioral change).

The assessment of the organizations involved document reviews, key informant interviews, direct observation, and staff surveys. The document review and interview components are constituted of in-depth interviews with management level staff, often including the executive/managing director, finance officer, human resources manager, information manager, and the storekeeper. During the interview and document review, the interviewee is asked to describe a process, document, plan, or strategy and then documentation or direct observation is used to verify the interviewee's responses. The staff survey assesses the staff members' knowledge of the organization and organizational functioning and processes in all the 11 domains (e.g., staff are asked if their NGO has a strategic plan, if they have discussed the annual plan in a meeting in the last 4 months, etc.). After the baseline assessment, we provided the organizations written feedback sent to them by email. The feedback outlined their scores in the different domains of the assessment, their areas of weakness, and the actionable steps they could take to improve their capacity. The organizations were then reassessed yearly for two years in Ethiopia; while, in Nigeria they were reassessed once after six months.

The results of the data collections demonstrated significant improvements in the overall development score for most organizations. However, there were organizations that did not improve or that declined in capacity. In Ethiopia, the change in the overall capacity of the NGOs after two years ranged from -11 to 25 percentage points, with a mean of 9; while, in Nigeria the change in capacity ranged from -6 to 59 percentage points, with a mean of 16. Based on the change in organizational capacity, we divided the NGOs into quartiles and we called the NGOs in the highest change quartile high-performing organizations and called those in the lowest quartile low-performing organizations. We were curious to know why there were marked differences in the changes that occurred in organizations. On further investigation, we discovered no significant differences in the age, budget, location, staff size, board size, and number of board meetings between the high- and low-performing organizations. There was also no significant difference in the external capacity building support received by the high- and low-performing organizations during the period of the study.

To better understand the marked differences in the changes we saw in the organizations, we further interviewed 76 of the executive directors (20 in Ethiopia and 56 in Nigeria). We asked them questions about what they did during the change process, what they felt helped them change, the challenges they faced, and how they overcame their challenges. Different organizations did different things after they received the assessment report, ranging from reviewing the report and doing nothing about it, to actively making plans on how to make a change. From our interviews and observations at the organizations, we discovered six main differences in the actions taken by the high-performing organizations and those by the low-performing organizations. We found that unlike most of the low-performing organizations, the high-performing organizations did these:

1. Created the right atmosphere for change (prepared the nest for the egg)

2. Had enthusiastic and motivated staff (staff were in high spirits)

3. Set goals (took steps toward turning the invisible into the visible)

4. Worked as a team (used the ants' strategy)

5. Were engaged in peer mentoring (showed each other the way)

6. Collaborated with other organizations (employed the power of synergy)

This book explains the six factors that helped these organizations to make a positive change in their capacity. It is further enriched by empirical evidence from other scholars that supports or further expands on how these six factors help organizations to achieve change. The names of the specific organizations are not mentioned in the book because I do not have the consent of the NGOs to use their names. However, when necessary, I explained characteristics of specific organizations for a better understanding of the actions they took. One interesting finding from this study is that change in organizations does not happen arbitrarily but is a result of diligent planning and action by organizations that believe that they can change and persevere in the change process even when such belief is contrary to current realities.

CHAPTER 2
PREPARING THE NEST FOR THE EGG

"Give me six hours to chop down a tree and I will spend the first four sharpening the axe."

— Abraham Lincoln

"Spectacular achievement is always preceded by unspectacular preparation."

— Robert H. Schuller

Growing up in the country side, I once observed a bird prepare her nest prior to laying eggs. She picked grasses and leaves from different places and sometimes flew great distances to drop them one after the other on the tree where she was building the nest. It was a slow and laborious process but it seemed as if she understood that the only way the eggs could be incubated properly is by having a well-built nest. She went on diligently and steadily until she finished the nest, laid the eggs, incubated the eggs, and got them transformed into young birds. Although the ultimate outcome was the young birds, the first step toward that outcome was diligently preparing the nest. It is a process that, though it might seem unimportant to the casual onlooker, is a fundamental and mandatory step for the eggs to become young birds. I saw the same process in all the organizations that accomplished great change. They took the time to create the right environment for change. Effective and progressive organizational growth will be difficult or even impossible if the appropriate climate for change is not created. However, most people will not want to change their set ways of doing things if they do not understand the need for change or if there is no major internal or external crisis that threatens their existence and acts as a trigger for change. [1] So, creating the right climate for organizational change can be equated to creating the right climate for effective and progressive organizational growth.

Change in organizations can be incremental (evolutionary) or transformational (revolutionary). Incremental or evolutionary changes are small changes that alter little of what the organization does or how the organization works without changing the main framework of the organization. These kinds of changes are usually easier to implement and engender less resistance to change. Examples of incremental change include adopting a new data management software, changing the account management system, etc. Transformational or revolutionary changes involve changes to the main framework of what the organization does or how the organization works. The impact of the change and the resistance to change are usually higher in transformational change. An example of transformational change is changing from a hierarchical management structure to self-directed work teams.

No matter the type of change, there can be resistance to change. Just like a body at rest will have inertia opposing movement unless it is acted upon by a force that overcomes the resistance to change, individuals and organizations resist change and do so for varied reasons. Resistance to change is not inherently wrong because not every change is good for an organization or individual. However, for any organization to make progress and be able to survive the dynamic external environment, there is need for managers to learn how to create the appropriate climate that will enable change and prevent resistance to change.

From our study, these were some of the main causes of resistance to change in organizations:

- Deeply rooted organizational values and culture - employees were very comfortable with the way they were already doing things and were very reluctant to learn new methods.
- Staff or management felt there was no need for change.
- Major stakeholders were not involved in making the decision about change.
- Staff or management or both felt change was not cost-effective.
- Staff or management or both felt change was not realistic or attainable.

- Staff or management or both felt they lacked the resources to effectively implement the change.

However, the focus of this chapter is not on analyzing why and how resistance to change occurs, neither is it on analyzing how to deal with resistance to change when it has occurred. Rather, the focus of this chapter is on how organizations can prepare the right environment for change and prevent resistance to change from occurring.

Practical steps that led to an environment conducive to change – experience from the field

From my experience working with 135 nonprofit organizations, I discovered that organizations that successfully made a change took steps that created the right environment for it. I saw these five steps in organizations that were successful in creating the right environment for change to improve their organizational capacity:

1. They had a shared understanding of the problem and need for change.
2. They had a shared understanding of how to accomplish the change.
3. They assigned specific tasks to specific people or teams.
4. They got support and feedback from management and staff.
5. They institutionalized the change.

Although 100% of the high-performing organizations in our study took all or most of these steps, 46% of the low-performing organizations also took some of the same steps. The fact that all high-performing organizations created the right environment for change shows that change might be practically impossible without creating the right environment for it. However, the fact that some of the low-performing organizations that took some of the same steps did not succeed in accomplishing the change they desired shows that though creating the right environment is very important, it is not the only necessary step.

Shared understanding of the problem and need for change - One characteristic of all high-performing organizations was that they had a shared understanding of the need for change and the implications of the change to the organization. They had several staff and management meetings where they discussed the capacity assessment report we sent to them, their strengths and weaknesses, the implications of the result for their organization, and the need for change. There was a shared understanding of the need for change among the staff and management.

This was contrary to what happened in some organizations that were not successful with their efforts to implement change. In one of the medium-sized organizations (for the purposes of this book, I will define a medium-sized organization as one with a staff size of 51 – 250) the executive director shared the report of the findings of the assessment with only members of the management team. This organization was one of the well-resourced organizations, had highly educated people on the management team, and implemented a more hierarchical organizational structure. The management team met (without input from other staff) and they did not all appreciate the magnitude of the problem or reach a consensus on the need for change. They took some steps to improve, but had little success. This can be partly attributed to lack of unity of purpose and pursuit.

Shared understanding of the steps to take - Apart from having a shared vision of the problem, the next step that worked for the organizations that successfully changed was having a shared understanding of the way to go about making that change. These high-performing organizations met as a team; got inputs from staff, management, and board; and decided on the most effective steps they would need to take in order to improve. They evaluated their alternatives and reached a consensus on the steps to take to improve. They also took the time to understand roles; clarify expectations; and decide on the expected inputs, outputs, and time frame to accomplish the change. This gave staff ownership of the change process. One of the executive directors told me that the most important factor that helped them not only to make changes, but to sustain the changes over time was involvement of the staff in having a shared understanding of the steps they needed to take. He said "We presented the assessment report to the general staff meeting. Then, we discussed it one by one, point by point, by domains. We discussed the weaknesses, strengths, high priorities, and low priorities. We agreed on the actions we needed to take. From that, all the staff were on the same page and on track to improve their performance." The main point here is that it is important for staff who will be directly involved in implementing a change process to have a shared understanding of the steps to take.

Assigned specific tasks to specific people/teams – After what to do was decided, staff were assigned specific responsibilities. In some organizations, committees were formed to spearhead different aspects of the change process. The committees reviewed the resources that were available to them and decided who will be responsible for doing what and the timeline for getting things done. I will like to tell the story of one of the two organizations that had the greatest improvement in organizational capacity in Ethiopia. The executive director of this 14 year old organization with 47 staff told me that the secret of the great improvement in their capacity was in assigning specific responsibility to staff after they had decided the best way to deal with the challenges. Interestingly, while the majority of the executive directors I interviewed had at least a master's degree, this executive director did not have a college degree. However, he knew how to get his staff involved in the change process and how to work with them to get outstanding results.

Support and feedback from staff and management - Starting the change process is great but concluding it is even more important. We had organizations where the change started and stopped mid-way due to a loss of enthusiasm for the change, a change in the organization's leadership, or an actual or perceived lack of resources to carry on with the change. Most of the teams that successfully implemented change were those that provided ongoing reports on progress and challenges and got feedback from staff and management. They were also the teams that had access to the resources they needed to accomplish their tasks. As one of the executive directors stated, regular feedback meetings were one of the most important things that helped her organization to improve. The meetings provided them with an opportunity for ongoing feedback and helped them remain enthusiastic and focused on the change in the midst of competing priorities. This organization, which just had 34 staff, met every two weeks to discuss progress and had one of the greatest improvements in capacity in Ethiopia. Additionally, they had over 300% increase in their finances within 2 years. The interesting thing about this organization was that the executive director was a quiet and humble woman, who did not appear very charismatic, but she knew how to get a team to work together and achieve great results.

Institutionalized changes – For the organizations we followed up for two years, we noticed that some made changes in the first year but by the second year they had reverted back to their former ways of doing things. The changes were not sustained. However, organizations that sustained change did things differently from those that did not sustain change. Some of the organizations that sustained change modified their policies and procedures to reflect the new way of doing things. In addition, they reinforced the new behaviors by rewarding those behaviors. In one of the high-performing organizations that sustained its change, the executive director constantly talked about the importance of the change they accomplished and openly praised the staff for their great commitment in making and sustaining the change. I believe this helped to reinforce the change and made the staff understand that sustaining the change is highly valued by the management.

Keys to creating an effective change climate in organizations

From review of the steps taken by the high-performing organizations, two pillars for creating an effective change climate became obvious; namely, effective communication and participative management (involving staff in decision-making in the organization). Participative management will be discussed under chapter 3. In this chapter, I will discuss effective communication that leads to organizational change and growth.

Effective communication that leads to change – what does the literature say?

There is no way staff can have a shared understanding of the problem or the solutions to the problem without effective communication. Therefore, we can say that a growing organization is an organization that has learned to communicate effectively. Additionally, a review of the factors that lead to resistance to change shows that most of them can be prevented by effective communication in organizations. The communication that I observed in these organizations mirrored Ford et al.'s (1995) four stages of effective communication: [2]

1. Conversation to initiate change – initiative conversation
2. Conversation to understand change – understanding conversation
3. Conversation to implement change – performance conversation
4. Conversation to conclude change – closure conversation

Initiative conversation (starting the change conversation) - This is conversation that is focused on letting people see the need for change. It is the time to highlight the external competition, environmental change, decline in the organization, or impending decline that warrants the change. It can also be a time to share a proactive vision of moving the organization forward in order for the organization to stay ahead of the competition. The initiative conversation can start in formal or informal meetings. It can come in the form of a suggestion from a member of staff on a needed change in the organization and why she or he thinks the change is needed. [2] In some of the organizations, the initiative conversation started immediately after the capacity assessment as the assessment made them aware of their deficiencies. However, for the majority of the organizations, receiving the assessment report that outlined the areas of their strengths and weaknesses and the steps needed for improvement triggered the initiative conversation. It was during the initiative conversation that most of the organizations had a shared understanding of the problem and need for change.

Understanding conversation (understanding the change) - This is the stage at which people try to understand the issues, problems, and opportunities. To review the evidence and examine the assumptions behind the thinking. It is also the time to generate and evaluate alternatives for overcoming the challenge and to reach a consensus on how to overcome the challenge. It is the time to set goals and decide the steps to take in order to accomplish those goals. [2] Additionally, it is the time to (1) specify the expected inputs, outcomes, and time frame of the process; and (2) specify those who will be directly or indirectly involved in the process. As much as is possible, the people who will be directly or indirectly involved in the process should be involved in the discussion. This stage is the time to understand roles, clarify expectations, and provide an opportunity for people to express their concerns, ideas, and suggestions. In summary, understanding conversation is the process of deciding what must be done, why, when, how, and by whom. It leads to the staff having a shared understanding of the steps they need to take to achieve change as we saw in the high-performing organizations in our study.

Performance conversation (getting into action) - This is the stage at which organizations request that people take specific actions. This may be a request for people to join a committee or to start keeping certain records, etc. The request may be accepted ("sure, I will be glad to join the committee"); declined ("sorry, I might not be able to join the committee now"); or negotiated with a counter offer ("I will be happy to join the committee but I will not be able to do that till February"). [2] One of the challenges in trying to change an organization is that people start having the performance conversation without first having the understanding conversation. If people do not first understand what should be done, why, when, and how it should be done (conversation for understanding), it becomes difficult for them to be motivated to carry out the required action. In our earlier discussion of the high-performing organizations, this was the stage when specific tasks were assigned to specific people or teams.

Closure conversation (ending the change process) - This is a time for appraisal, appreciation, celebration of results and accomplishments, and declaration of the change process terminated or completed. It also involves conversation on the way forward for the organization. [2] In our study, this was the time the organizations started having conversations on institutionalizing the change.

Causes and prevention of change communication failure

I discovered that there were failures in change communication at its various stages that affected the ability of organizations to implement change. This is in agreement with Ford et al. (1995) that communication failure can occur at each stage of the communication chain which could hamper the start, implementation, or continuation of change. [2]

Initiative conversation

Causes of initiative conversation failure – In our study, initiative communication failed when executive directors failed to agree there was a problem that needed attention. In one of the low-performing organizations, the executive director felt that the organization was doing okay and that the assessment report was not a true reflection of the organization. Once he expressed that sentiment, it ended any further discussion on the need for improvement. In another organization, the executive director said that there was no immediate monetary benefit of making any change and did not encourage any further discussion on the need for capacity improvement of the organization. As is the case in these two organizations, employees might not start initiative conversations if they sense that a supervisor is not willing to have that conversation or if they feel that their past initiative conversations have been ignored, opposed, or dismissed. In addition, when people are afraid of being judged harshly or unfavorably for their suggestions, they might not start initiative conversations. Furthermore, even if the change conversation is initiated, it might fail if the conversation is among people who cannot or who feel they cannot do anything about the problem or issue. [2] For instance, when a staff in the accounts department tells the monitoring and evaluation manager what he feels needs to be changed in the accounts department, the monitoring and evaluation manager might not do anything about it because he is not in charge of the accounts department. This kind of communication failure happens in organizations where people are not aware of the right people they need to talk to if they have a problem, complaint, or suggestion. Surprisingly, I discovered that there were staff in the organizations we worked with who were not aware of the right persons to talk to if they had a complaint or suggestion in the organization.

How to prevent initiative conversation failure – Managers should understand that their words and body languages matter a lot in organizations. When a manager expresses his opinion early, it can make staff who have contrary opinions not to express their opinions even if their opinions are superior to that of the manager. Managers should learn not to quickly express their opinions about issues but allow and encourage staff to voice their opinions and suggestions first. Any organization that values change and growth must encourage its staff to come up with ideas on how to improve. Additionally, managers should ensure that any suggestion for change or improvement is acknowledged as valued and staff are rewarded for bringing up ideas for change that are successfully implemented. This reward can be financial (e.g. cash bonus) or non-financial (e.g. praise). In organizations where change and innovation are not valued, staff might not be willing to start conversations about change. Furthermore, managers should create a safe environment in their organizations where people are not afraid to make mistakes and where staff and their views are respected. Additionally, managers should ensure staff are aware of the right people to talk to if they have a problem, complaint, or suggestion.

Understanding conversation

Causes of understanding conversation failure – In our study, understanding communication failed when managers had already decided what to do and closed any avenue for input from other staff. In one of the low-performing organizations, the staff reached a consensus during the initiative conversation that there was need for improvement in the organization. However, the conversation for change could not progress because the executive director expressed that the organization was unable to change due to lack of an external capacity-building fund. This stopped staff from making suggestions on how they could overcome the financial constraint and improve their organizational capacity. In another organization, the executive director agreed that there was need for change, but felt that it should be discussed later because the organization had other competing priorities. Unfortunately, the enthusiasm that came with the capacity assessment and feedback fizzled out and the understanding conversation never took place. Understanding communication might also fail when there is no shared understanding of the problem, solution, and expected outcome in the organization. [2] It can fail when the manager does not give adequate time for discussion of the change process. Furthermore, understanding conversation can be said to have failed if it does not lead to a specific and focused expected outcome. [3] If the conversation fails in making people understand what must be done, why, when, how, and by whom then understanding communication can be said to have failed.

How to prevent understanding communication failure – Managers should work with the mood of the staff and ensure that opportunities for positive change are utilized when there is enthusiasm for change among the staff. Postponing a discussion when the right opportunity presents itself (such as after capacity assessment and feedback in our study) might lead to that discussion never happening again. Furthermore, understanding communication thrives in organizations where staff are given the opportunity to express their views and made to understand that their views matter. In addition to involving staff in decision-making, the manager should give enough time for discussion and should be open to accepting the input from the staff. To ensure that conversations are focused, moderators of such discussions should outline the main points to be discussed in each meeting and make sure that at the end of the discussions people are clear on what should be done, why, when, how, and by whom.

Performance communication

Causes of performance communication failure - Understanding and agreeing on what should be done is not enough to bring about the performance of what is agreed. [4] There should be a specific assignment of roles and responsibilities that makes people accountable for specific outcomes. So, stopping the conversation after people have understood the what, why, when, how, and by whom is insufficient. There should be clear and definite assignment of roles and responsibilities.

However, assigning specific roles or making a specific demand for action might not succeed if there is no time limit for the task. [2] I saw from our study that telling staff to finish a task as soon as possible might lead to that task not being done due to other competing priorities that have specific deadlines. So the assigned task should not only be clear and specific, it should have a specified timeline.

In addition, making unreasonable requests can be another reason for an unsuccessful change process. [5] Telling people to do what they do not have the skills or resources to do or asking people to do things within an unrealistic time frame might be reasons for an unsuccessful change process.

How to prevent performance communication failure – Managers should ensure that tasks are assigned to specific people or teams and that a realistic time frame is set for each task. In addition, employees and teams should be provided with the resources and training they need to succeed.

Closure communication

Closure Conversation - Lack of a conversation for closure is another reason why change might be unsuccessful. There is a need to appreciate people for their efforts and to end the project or discuss why the deadline was not met and what the next steps are. Lack of closure may make people feel that their efforts are not appreciated and valued and may make them less enthusiastic to be part of another project. From my experience, the main cause of closure communication failure is lack of awareness of its importance. Closure communication was one of the differences I saw between organizations that had a sustainable change (by institutionalizing the change) and those that did not.

Chapter summary

Setting up an environment conducive to change is a necessary part of organizational growth.

Practical steps that lead to change include these:

- Having a shared understanding of the problem and need for change
- Having a shared understanding of how to accomplish the change
- Assigning specific tasks to specific people or teams
- Getting support and feedback from management and staff for teams that are pioneering the change
- Institutionalizing the change

There are two pillars for creating an effective change climate:

- Effective communication
- Participative management (involving staff in decision-making in the organization)

Effective communication that leads to change is in four parts:

- Conversation to initiate change – initiative conversation
- Conversation to understand change – understanding conversation

- Conversation to implement change – performance conversation
- Conversation to conclude change – closure conversation

These are some of the causes of change communication failure:

- Failure to initiate change conversation because past initiative conversation was ignored, opposed, or dismissed.
- Failure to initiate change conversation due to fear of being judged harshly or unfavorably for suggestion.
- Change conversation being among people who cannot do anything about the problem or issue.
- Lack of a shared understanding of the problem, solution, and expected outcome.
- Inadequate time for discussion of the change process.
- Lack of specific and focused expected outcome.
- Lack of understanding of what must be done, why, when, how, and by whom.
- No clear and definite assignment of roles and responsibilities.
- No specified timeline for assigned roles.
- Roles assigned to people who do not have the skills or resources to accomplish them.

How to prevent change communication failure:

- Staff should be rewarded for bringing up ideas for change that are successfully implemented.
- Managers should treat staff with respect.

- Managers should ensure people are aware of the right persons they need to talk to if they have a problem, complaint, or suggestion.
- Staff should be involved in major decision-making about the change.
- Managers should create enough time for discussion about proposed change.
- Managers should ensure that at the end of the discussion staff are clear on what will be done, why, when, how, and by whom.
- Managers should ensure that tasks are assigned to specific people or teams.
- Tasks should have a specific and realistic time frame.
- Staff should be provided with the resources and training they need to succeed.

CHAPTER 3
GETTING THE STAFF IN HIGH SPIRITS

"With an enthusiastic team you can achieve almost anything"

—Tahir Shah

"Enthusiasm spells the difference between mediocrity and accomplishment."

— Norman Vincent Peale

I will start this chapter by describing two organizations I visited in Addis Ababa, Ethiopia. These organizations were similar in a lot of ways. Both had their headquarters in Addis Ababa, both were serving orphans and vulnerable children, both were run by executive directors who were founders of the organization, and both had similar budget and staff sizes. However, one thing clearly differentiated them, the enthusiasm the staff showed when our team visited them to reassess their capacity. For one of the organizations, which tremendously improved its capacity, I easily saw the excitement among the staff and the feeling of a sense of achievement. While, for the other organization, which had little capacity improvement, it appeared as if our visit was a burden to the organization. These were not isolated cases; as, over and over again, I discovered that highly enthusiastic and motivated staff was one of the features of high-performing organizations. These enthusiastic and highly motivated staff were ready and willing to go above their call of duty to ensure that their organizations improved. I will define motivation as the force, intrinsic or extrinsic, that drives people to behave in certain ways or perform certain tasks in order to achieve personal or organizational goals. Thus, a motivated person is one who is energized toward a goal while an unmotivated person is one who feels no impetus or inspiration to act. [1] Motivation can be intrinsic or extrinsic:

Intrinsic motivation - Intrinsic motivation is when people are internally driven to behave in certain ways or perform certain activities because they find them interesting and derive fulfillment from doing them. There are several things that enhance intrinsic motivation, one of which is the feeling of competence, autonomy, and purpose. Furthermore, staff performing an optimally challenging task and receiving positive feedback enhances intrinsic motivation by enhancing their feelings of competence. [2] In addition, involving staff in decision-making and giving staff tasks that align with their personal interests, vision, and purposes leads to their intrinsic motivation.

Extrinsic motivation - Conversely, extrinsic motivation is when people are driven to perform certain activities, not because they find them interesting or derive fulfillment from such activities, but because of the extrinsic rewards--such as tangible rewards or verbal praise--that come from such activities. [2] Apart from tangible rewards and verbal praise, deadlines, supervision, and evaluation are other extrinsic motivators.

Importance of staff motivation

From our experience staff motivation leads to these:

- Greater staff commitment and productivity
- Increased customer or client satisfaction
- Increased probability of survival of the organization

Signs of unmotivated staff

While the focus of this chapter is not on identifying signs of job dissatisfaction and demotivation, it will be important to point out some of the signs of demotivation seen in previous studies. They include the following: [3]

- High job turnover
- Absenteeism
- Lateness to work
- Low job performance
- Grievances at work
- Drug abuse
- Unionization
- Decision to retire

Attributes of organizations with motivated and enthusiastic staff – Experience from the field

The important question is why are staff in some organizations more excited, committed, and motivated than staff in other organizations. I do not presume to have the encompassing answer to this question, but while talking with the executive directors and staff in some of the organizations we worked with, I was able to learn some key differences between organizations that had motivated and enthusiastic staff and those that did not. I discovered six factors in organizations where I saw enthusiasm and commitment from staff:

- Challenging roles and responsibilities
- Involvement in decision-making
- Sense of purpose and fulfilment
- Sense of community
- Culture of the organization
- Expectation of reward

Challenging roles and responsibility – One attribute that I noticed in high-performing organizations in which the staff appeared enthusiastic was that staff were given challenging responsibilities and key roles to play in the capacity building process. In one of the organizations, the staff acted as internal consultants as specific staff were given roles to lead capacity improvement in different areas. They were to build expertise and lead the improvement process in specific areas; tasks that the staff felt were challenging but yet exciting. During the reassessment of the organizational capacity of one of the organizations with enthusiastic staff, the executive director played a passive role and allowed the staff who had become "technical experts" in the different organizational capacity components to lead the discussion.

Involvement in decision-making – Another factor that I noticed in the organizations with increased enthusiasm was involvement of the staff in the decision-making process of the organizations. One example of staff involvement was the executive directors involving the staff in responding to our question on their organizations' three greatest areas of strength and weakness. I observed that in some organizations, the executive directors sought input from other staff who were around on what they felt were their three greatest strengths and weaknesses, while in others, the executive directors just provided the answer. What I noticed to be similar in organizations where the staff were involved in providing this answer was that they seemed more engaged and enthusiastic about the change.

Sense of purpose and fulfilment – An executive director of one of the organizations with enthusiastic staff told me that the major driving force of the staff commitment I saw in her organization was the staff's sense of purpose and fulfilment in spending their lives doing something that was worthwhile – serving and advocating for poor and vulnerable populations. She said that the staff saw the capacity building as an effort to help them get better at doing the job they love to do, and so it was easy for them to commit to it. She had worked purposefully and consistently over the years to build a sense of pride and self-fulfillment in the staff, in the job they do. She said "most of the employees are not just working to make a living, because, the things we are doing are much more than that. They are changing the lives of people and living beyond themselves. So, they have this understanding, which is what makes us unique." This idea was also echoed by other nonprofit organizations who said that what had kept most of their staff in the organization was not the salary, which was usually not very competitive, but the sense of purpose and fulfillment in the staff.

Sense of community – the feeling of a sense of belonging and friendship in the organization was one of the attributes of organizations in which staff were enthusiastic about the capacity building. In one high-performing organization in Ethiopia with 28 staff at the headquarters and 104 staff nationally, the female executive director and founder, who had been in-charge of the organization for 15 years, created an opportunity for staff to have lunch together. She created a subsidized lunch program in which staff contribute a subsidized amount of money each month for group lunch. Lunch time created an opportunity for informal interactions between staff and management. It also created an opportunity for board members, funders, and visitors to occasionally interact with staff and management over lunch. That program tremendously helped staff to interact and become friends across departments and it built a sense of community in the whole organization. It also made staff connected to the organization and made them feel they were major stakeholders in the organization and in its capacity development.

Culture of the organization – the culture of the organization also affected the enthusiasm for change. I found more enthusiasm for change in organizations that had a culture of excellence, change, and continuous improvement. I discovered that organizations where they already had structures in place for continuous improvement--such as peer training sessions and quality improvement review sessions--were more enthusiastic for change compared to organizations where such structures did not exist. Additionally, organizations that had a culture of external competition, that always wanted to be better than their peers, were also more enthusiastic about change than those that did not have such a culture.

Expectation of reward – Although the capacity assessment was not a precursor to a specific grant funding, the organizations that felt that making the changes will help them attract more funds were more enthusiastic about change. This was opposite to what I saw in some of the low-performing organizations who were not enthusiastic for change. In one of the organizations, the executive director said that he knew that the capacity building was not directly linked to obtaining a grant and felt it was a waste of their time: "so actually we were concerned about the time we were going to invest in this capacity building. If it is not bringing in any grants for the organization it might not be worth it; but, we just decided to do it." The executive director of another low-performing organization where we noticed lack of enthusiasm about improving their organization said that they participated in the capacity assessment because they did not want to disappoint two of their funders who wanted them to participate in the program, and not because they were really eager to improve.

What leads to staff motivation? – What the literature says

There are several theories that explain what motivates people to put in their best to achieve a desired goal. Some of these theories include the Maslow theory of human motivation, Frederick Herzberg's hygiene-motivation theory, Vroom's expectancy theory, Adams' equity theory, and Skinner's reinforcement theory. Although an in-depth discussion of these theories is beyond the scope of this book, I will briefly explain some of these theories in order for managers to better understand how they can utilize them to improve the motivation of their employees.

Maslow's theory of human motivation and how it applies to managers

Maslow hypothesized that there are five levels of hierarchy of need: [4]

- Physiological needs
- Safety needs
- Love or social needs
- Esteem needs

- Self-actualization needs

Physiological needs - This is the base level of the hierarchy of need and the most important to man. This is man's desire to satisfy the basic needs of life such as food, clothing, and housing. When these are not satisfied, they become the greatest motivator of man's action. For someone who is hungry, the most important thing that matters to him is to satisfy the hunger. However, when the hunger has been consistently satisfied, the physiological need no longer becomes a motivator of behavior. [4] Therefore, wages and salaries will be great motivators as far as the employees are still struggling to meet their physiological needs.

Safety needs - When physiological needs are satisfied, at least to a reasonable extent, the safety or security needs become the most dominant motivator of behavior. Man desires some protection from uncertainties, danger, deprivation, and threats. At this level, job security becomes a major motivator for the employees. The employees feel insecure in an environment where management takes arbitrary and unpredictable actions that threaten employees' jobs. They also feel insecure where there is uncertainty about their continued employment or the continued existence of the company, or, where there is favoritism or discrimination. [4]

Social or love needs - When the physiological and safety needs of man are reasonably satisfied, then the need for acceptance, association, belongingness, and affection (both giving and receiving affection) becomes the most paramount. Thus, the relationship of staff with their peers, subordinates, and supervisors becomes the main motivator of behavior after physiological and safety needs are met. Having a workgroup where the staff are friends, respect and care about each other, and feel they are loved can be a strong motivator. However, some managers are afraid of a cohesive workforce and do not encourage it due to the fear that it can also be a strong force to resist management. Managing a cohesive workforce well can be to the advantage of the organization as it will be more effective and will achieve more compared to separate individuals working alone. [4]

Esteem or ego needs - Esteem or ego need is the next level of need that motivates behavior. It becomes pre-eminent when the prior levels of need have been reasonably satisfied. Unlike the previous levels of need, the esteem needs cannot be fully satisfied. The esteem needs are at two levels. The first is the desire for knowledge, achievement, self-confidence, independence, freedom, and expertise. The second is the need for reputation – this includes need for appreciation, recognition, prestige, status, and respect from others. [4]

Self-actualization or self-fulfillment needs - This is the need to be self-fulfilled in what the employee is doing. This is the employees' desires to be the best they can possibly be and to continue to self-develop. This varies from person to person and becomes important when other levels of need have been reasonably satisfied. [4]

Implications for managers

Managers should understand that as employees' lower levels of need are met, fulfilling those needs no longer motivates employees' behaviors. So the fact that employees are paid competitive salaries and fringe benefits and provided excellent working conditions and job security does not mean that they will be motivated to put in their best for the organization. As the physiological and safety needs are met, they no longer become motivators for achievement. This was very true in our study as I saw over and over again that the thing that staff identified as their major source of motivation was not their salaries, but rather, things like the sense of friendship and community they felt in the organization and the opportunity they had to spend their lives doing what they were passionate about, among others.

If management only focuses on meeting employees' physiological and safety needs, the employees might still be dissatisfied and might keep making more demands for improved working conditions in the erroneous belief that further increase in wages will deal with their dissatisfaction. [4] Managers must ensure that employees' needs for association, independence, recognition, status, belongingness, and appreciation are fulfilled. Managers might not be able to provide their employees with self-fulfillment or self-esteem but they should be able to create the conditions that allow the employees to develop and fulfill those needs for themselves.

Frederick Herzberg's hygiene-motivation theory

Frederick Herzberg's hygiene-motivation theory is related to Maslow's theory of motivation. It also asserts that man has several needs that if met or not met will lead to job satisfaction or dissatisfaction. However, Herzberg argued that job dissatisfaction is not the opposite of job satisfaction. [5] He stated that the opposite of job satisfaction is no job satisfaction and that the opposite of job dissatisfaction is no job dissatisfaction. This, he argued, is because the factors that lead to job satisfaction are quite different from those that cause job dissatisfaction. Table 1 shows Herzberg's causes of job satisfaction and dissatisfaction.

Table 1: Causes of Job Satisfaction and Job Dissatisfaction

Cause of job satisfaction	Causes of job dissatisfaction
Achievement	Company policy and administration
Recognition for achievement	Supervision
The work itself	Interpersonal relationship
Responsibility	Working conditions
Growth or advancement	Salary
	Status
	Security

The implication of the theory is that a good manager will not only deal with things that will lead to staff dissatisfaction but will also focus on things that will lead to satisfaction.

How to reduce job dissatisfaction

Herzberg outlined several conditions that affect job dissatisfaction. [5] Fulfilling these conditions will reduce job dissatisfaction while not meeting the conditions will lead to job dissatisfaction. The conditions that will reduce job dissatisfaction include the following:

- Company policies that are supportive and not obstructive
- Supervision that is effective, supportive, respectful, and non-judgmental
- Good workplace interpersonal relationships
- Good working conditions
- Good and competitive wages
- Meaningful job schedules for each position
- Job security

How to improve job satisfaction

Herzberg opined that reducing job dissatisfaction by providing good wages, good job security, and a good work environment is not enough to cause job satisfaction and motivate staff to increase their productivity. He outlined factors that will lead to job satisfaction: [5]

- Providing people opportunities to do something meaningful and achieve great results

- Recognizing people for their achievements and contributions
- Giving people work they find challenging but achievable based on their skills and abilities
- Giving people responsibility that makes them feel they are important to the organization
- Giving people opportunity to grow in knowledge, skill, work responsibility, and position in the company

Implication of Herzberg's theory for managers

There are several steps managers can take to reduce job dissatisfaction and improve job satisfaction. These include the following:

Job enrichment - Herzberg advocates for job enrichment as a way of motivating staff and improving their psychological growth. Job enrichment, distinct from job enlargement, is not increasing the quantity of the same work an employee is doing (horizontal increase) but rather increasing the responsibility of the employee (vertical increase). Job enrichment includes encouraging staff to take up new and challenging responsibilities; assigning specific and specialized tasks to employees that will help them become subject matter experts; granting extra authority to employees and giving them some room to use their initiative; increasing employees accountability by making the employees, and not their supervisors, accountable for the quality and accuracy of their work; allowing employees to sign off on some documents on behalf of the organization; and providing employees opportunities to represent the organization in their areas of specialty. This was true in our study as I saw a lot of enthusiasm in organizations where staff were given roles as internal consultants and technical experts in different capacity areas and allowed to lead the organizational change in those areas.

Delegation of duties - Managers must learn to delegate duties and give more responsibilities to subordinates. This will satisfy the esteem needs of the employees and will make them feel important in the organization. Such employees will be motivated to put in their best. I spoke to a female executive director of a high-performing organization in Ethiopia who was a perfectionist and previously tried to supervise every major activity in her organization. She told me that the turning point in their organizational growth was when she learned to delegate duties to subordinates, allow them to make mistakes, and support them to excel in those tasks. I also noticed that some low-performing organizations concentrated much power in the executive director or a few managers and did not delegate enough responsibilities to others. This, I learned, was mainly due to a lack of trust in the abilities and capabilities of their staff. One sure way managers can facilitate growth in their staff is by giving them challenging responsibilities and supporting them to succeed. Managers must accept that employees will make mistakes before they can perfect their skills and so should be patient and support them in the learning process.

Participatory management - Participatory management is another way for managers to improve the job satisfaction of employees. As we saw in chapter two, participatory management is also important in creating the right atmosphere for change in organizations. Participatory management is the practice of involving both managers and employees in information processing, decision-making, and problem solving. It leads to sharing of influence between the managers and their subordinates. [6] Participatory management is associated with job satisfaction, improved employee productivity, and increased employee commitment. [6-8] As I saw in our study, involving the staff in deciding the importance of change and the steps to take to accomplish the desired change was a characteristic of all high-performing organizations.

Vroom's expectancy theory

Vroom's expectancy theory states that employees are motivated to work hard based on their belief that their efforts will result in outcomes which will be positively rewarded. [9] The size of the reward is directly related to the level of motivation. For example, if employees learn, believe, or perceive that attracting a new grant to the organization will lead to promotion or reward, they will put in a lot of effort to attract grants to the organization. If they are rewarded for their efforts, it will boost their morale to work harder to attract more grants. However, if they do not receive the reward they anticipated, they will be discouraged from working harder. As we saw in our study, lack of expectation of a positive reward from capacity development led to lack of staff enthusiasm for improving their capacity.

Implication for managers

Managers should clearly let employees know what they need to do to get a bonus, promotion, reward, or praise. This will motivate employees to work hard toward it. However, managers should ensure that the rewards are fulfilled once the staff attain the goals.

Adams' equity theory

Adams' equity theory states that employees strive for equity between themselves and other workers. [10,11] A feeling of equity in the workplace can be motivating while a feeling of inequity can be very demoralizing. There could be a loss of morale if staff feel that they do not get equitable pay, praise, or punishment for their actions. When staff feel that there is favoritism or victimization at the workplace, it leads to loss of morale. Employees' perception of distributive justice (fairness in the distribution of tasks and rewards); procedural justice (fairness in the process or procedure used to achieve an outcome); and interactional justice (fairness in interpersonal treatment by managers) increases job satisfaction. [12]

Implication for managers

Staff should be paid and treated equitably irrespective of their age, gender, race, or disability. Managers should ensure that there is distributive, procedural, and interactional justice at the workplace. They can do this by having a written and comprehensive employees' manual that states work ethics, procedures, expectations, and rewards which will be implemented across the board in the organization. One female executive director in Nigeria told me that prior to developing a comprehensive employees' manual, she had issues with low staff morale among some staff that felt they were unfairly treated. She spent a lot of time dealing with staff issues as there were no uniform standards to apply to different situations. She said that though preparing a human resources manual was time consuming, the gains from it far outweighed the resources they spent in preparing it as it made for easier and equitable handling of staff issues and less complaints of inequitable treatment and resulting low staff morale. Additionally, managers should also equitably appreciate the efforts of their employees because if employees feel that managers are not equally appreciating their work, it could also lead to loss of morale.

Skinner's reinforcement theory

Skinner's reinforcement theory states that employees' behaviors that lead to positive outcomes are reinforced and will be repeated and behaviors that lead to negative outcomes are not reinforced and will not be repeated. [10,13] Success motivates more action and failure leads to less action. So if an employee is praised or rewarded for meeting a particular target, such an employee will be motivated to repeat the actions that led to the outcome and vice versa.

Implication for managers

Managers should ensure that they praise and reward (positively reinforce) actions or results that will boost the achievement of the organization's goals and condemn or punish (negatively re-inforce) actions or outcomes that are contrary to achieving the organization's goals. However, as we saw in Adam's theory, such positive or negative reinforcement should be equitably done for it to achieve its purpose. One way to ensure equity is by incorporating such rewards or punishments in the human resources manual (or workers handbook) and institutionalizing them to ensure consistency in their application.

Chapter summary

Motivation is the force, intrinsic or extrinsic, that drives people to behave in certain ways or perform certain tasks in order to achieve personal or organizational goals.

Importance of staff motivation:

- Greater staff commitment and productivity
- Increased client or customer satisfaction

- Increased probability of survival of the organization

Attributes of organizations with motivated and enthusiastic staff:

- Challenging roles and responsibility
- Involvement in decision-making
- Sense of purpose and fulfilment
- Sense of community
- Culture of change in the organization
- Expectation of reward for positive action

How to motivate staff:

- Progressively meet staff's physiological, safety, social, esteem, and self-actualization needs.
- Provide staff opportunities to do something meaningful and achieve great results.
- Recognize staff for their achievements and contributions.
- Give staff work they find challenging but achievable based on their skills and abilities.
- Give staff responsibilities that make them feel they are important to the organization.
- Give staff opportunities to grow in knowledge, skill, work responsibility, and position in the company.
- Delegate duties to staff.
- Involve staff in major decision-making.

- Meet staff's expectations that their input will lead to a desirable outcome.
- Ensure equity and fairness at the workplace.
- Reinforce positive behavior.

How to prevent job dissatisfaction (Frederick Herzberg's hygiene-motivation theory):

- Company policies that are supportive and not obstructive
- Supervision that is effective, supportive, respectful, and non-judgmental
- Good workplace interpersonal relationships
- Good working conditions
- Good and competitive wages
- Meaningful job schedules for each position
- Job security

CHAPTER 4
TURNING THE INVISIBLE INTO THE VISIBLE

"Setting goals is the first step in turning the invisible into the visible"

– Tony Robbins

"If you set your goals ridiculously high and it's a failure, you will fail above everyone else's success"

– James Cameron

In the first phase of our work with nonprofit organizations in Ethiopia, I discovered that most organizations had a desire to grow and achieve great results but only a few set specific goals to help them achieve those desires. Additionally, fewer organizations persisted in working on their goals in the midst of challenges. We discovered that one key difference between high- and low-performing organizations was in planning for change. Organizations that had a plan with specific targets, timelines for achieving the goals, and individuals or groups responsible for the targets did significantly better. Due to the effect of goal setting we observed in Ethiopia, we sent all nonprofit organizations in

Nigeria a capacity development plan template to enable them plan and set specific goals for capacity building. The template contained columns for gaps identified for each assessed organizational capacity indicator, the specific activities they will take to correct the gaps, the person(s) that will be responsible, the resources needed, and the timeline for accomplishing the change. We noticed that on average, the nonprofit organizations in Nigeria (the second phase of our project) did better than those in Ethiopia (the first phase) by 10 percentage points. The greater improvement in Nigeria was notwithstanding the fact that the organizations in Nigeria had significantly less time to build their capacity compared to those in Ethiopia. Although other factors could have influenced the greater capacity improvement in organizations in Nigeria compared to those in Ethiopia, we believe that the capacity development plan template played a significant role. It helped organizations think through the specific actions they needed to take, the resources they needed to accomplish the tasks, and the specific timelines for action.

In this chapter, I will discuss the importance of goal setting, the characteristics of goals that will motivate staff, and the way to make goal setting effective in improving productivity.

Importance of goal setting

Setting goals has been shown to be very helpful to individuals and organizations. These are some of the advantages of goal setting: [1]

- Goals help to direct attention and effort to activities that are relevant to achieving the goal and away from irrelevant activities.
- Goals energize people for action. The higher the goal, the more the effort people put in.
- Goals encourage persistence. Having a goal makes people to persist to accomplish it.
- Goals encourage innovation. Goals make people discover or use task relevant knowledge and strategies.
- Goals lead to increased productivity.
- Goals help individuals and teams to self-regulate and self-manage their performance.

Characteristics of motivating goals – what the literature says

Goals have to be clear, challenging, achievable, rewarding, and simple in order to motivate people to take action to achieve them.

Clear and specific – Clear and specific goals are more effective than ambiguous or vague goals in motivating people to increase productivity. [2] In our study, organizations that set specific goals and assigned duties to specific people or committees performed better. Organizations that discussed the problems and decided that there was need to improve but did not set specific and clear goals did not improve much.

Challenging - Goals must be challenging enough to motivate people to strive hard to achieve them. [2] Goals that are easy to achieve might make people happy but will not bring out the best in people. Difficult goals motivate people to innovate and strive to learn new ways of effectively and efficiently dealing with challenges. However, the main issue is how to set goals that are appropriately challenging. There are several possible ways. One is to look at what is obtainable in the industry and set goals based on the standard of practice or the best results seen in the industry or any other standard related to what is happening in the industry (benchmarking). Another option is to look internally at the organization and set the goal based on the best outputs that the organization has had. A third option is for the employees and manager to decide on what is a challenging but attainable goal. The advantage of this is that the employees take ownership of the goals and will more clearly understand the goal right from the onset. A fourth option is for the management or board to set the goals for the organization or employees. [3]

Achievable - Although the goals should be challenging, they also have to be achievable. The main reason people give up on their goals is that the goals are not attainable with their best efforts. [2] One way to deal with this is to reassess the goals and set new and more realistic goals based on available resources. Another option is to see if there is need to improve the available knowledge, skills, and resources in order to achieve the goals. The problem might be that staff need training or additional resources in order to achieve the goals.

Rewarding - The attainment of the goal should lead to a reward that staff care about. The reward can be internal (pride, sense of achievement) or external (award, praise, monetary bonus, time off). Lack of a reward attached to attaining a goal is another reason why people give up on goals. In line with the expectancy theory of motivation, people are motivated to work hard when they believe that their work will lead to achieving their goals and that achieving those goals will directly or indirectly lead to personal benefits that they care about, such as personal pride, monetary reward, recognition, praise, time off, among others.

Simple - The more complex tasks are, the less effective the motivational effect of goal setting. Complex tasks are defined as tasks that require attending to several parts simultaneously, tasks that require coordinating several acts simultaneously, and tasks that have unpredictable changes in acts and information cues which place a big burden on individuals to adapt to the changes. [4]

How to make goal setting effective in improving productivity

Goals can be set by management with or without the input of staff. The most important thing is that there is a goal. Staff will usually do any work assigned to them whether they were part of the decision-making or not. However, involving the staff in setting the goals has added advantages. Locke et al noted that involving staff lead to a setting of higher goals and a better understanding of the purposes of the goals. [2] In my work with non-profit organizations, I observed that the organizations that made the greatest improvements in their capacity were those organizations that involved the staff and other stakeholders in setting their goals and drawing out plans on how to achieve those goals. Involving the staff in decision-making leads to having diverse inputs from staff on how to solve a particular problem which could be very helpful. In order to make goals succeed, the following are necessary:

Public commitment to the goal - Making a public commitment to a goal has been shown to make people more committed to achieving the goal. A manager or team that makes a public commitment to a goal will be more likely to achieve it than another manager or team that does not. [1] This is because public commitment makes the team to see achieving the goal as a matter of integrity.

Break up big goals into smaller goals - Goal setting is less effective in driving action when the task is complex. [1] However, when the complex goal is broken up into smaller proximal goals, goal setting becomes more effective in driving people to take action. [1] Having small wins motivates people to pursue bigger goals. For instance, a team might have a target of interacting with 1000 stakeholders in one year. Setting out weekly and monthly targets and celebrating success at the end of each month will be the way to go. Success in achieving the small goals reinforces the drive to achieve the bigger goal.

Furthermore, the goals people set depend on their previous performances and self-efficacy. People generally set goals to surpass their previous performance. So being able to achieve a previous goal motivates people to set a higher goal. [5] In the previous example, being able to meet a goal of interacting with 100 stakeholders in the first month, will most likely make the team set a higher goal the second month.

Improve self-efficacy and capacity to attain goal - Having goals might not lead to increased performance if people view them as threatening. Goals seen in a positive way, as a challenge, are more likely to be achieved than goals that are negatively viewed, as a threat. Goals are seen as challenging when they provide opportunity for growth and the individuals have strategies to cope with the stress of trying to achieve the goal. Conversely, goals are considered threatening when they are perceived to lead to failure with no available strategy to cope with them. [5]

People will be more committed to achieving a goal if they feel they have the knowledge, skills, and capacity to achieve the goal. Managers can improve the self-efficacy of their employees by (1) ensuring they have the resources, knowledge, and training they need to accomplish their tasks; (2) expressing confidence in the ability of the staff or team to achieve its goals; and (3) being role models or finding role models that staff can identify with. [1]

Provide supportive feedback - Providing support and feedback to employees is a great way of seeing that goals are accomplished; because, if people are not aware of how well they are doing, it becomes difficult for them to adjust their efforts and strategies to meet their goals. [1,6] One of the characteristics I found in high-performing organizations in our study is that they had regular meetings to review progress and provide supportive feedback to people who were working on different tasks. Colleagues also informally provided ideas and feedback on how to deal with problems. Thus, to facilitate achieving goals in organizations, managers should not only create an avenue for constant feedback but also encourage staff to speak up or ask questions when struggling with any task.

Build up enthusiasm for the goal - Commitment and enthusiasm for the goal are important for the realization of a goal. There are a lot of things that affect goal commitment and enthusiasm. Some of them include an awareness of the reward in achieving the goal; healthy competition between people or teams in the organization or between the organization and others (organizations should not set up formal competition between staff or teams in the organization as it may stifle the spirit of teamwork in the organization); and supportive and non-judgmental supervisors. [3]

Reduce goal conflicts - Group goals can be stalled when there is a conflict between personal and group goals. Groups perform best when personal goals align with group goals. [1,5] One way managers can reduce goal conflicts is to ensure that the reward system encourages the attainment of the goal. For instance, if people are rewarded for individual efforts in a teamwork, it will make them to be more interested in their individual success than in the team success.

Persevering in the goal – experience from the field

In our study, goal setting helped organizations achieve their missions. However, we discovered that not all the organizations that set goals were able to accomplish the goals. Some organizations had challenges that made it difficult for them to achieve their goals. Even so, the goal setting process made them understand the limitations they had and start thinking early about how to overcome the challenges. In my interviews with these organizations, I noted some of the challenges they faced in achieving their capacity building goals:

- Lack of capacity building funds – the organizations complained that most donors were not interested in capacity building. Donors' focuses were mainly on programs and they regarded capacity building funds as administrative costs which must be kept as low as possible.

- Inability to employ or retain high quality staff – the organizations complained of their inability to attract highly qualified and experienced personnel because they lack the funds to pay them. Similarly, they also had high staff turnover because their wages were not very competitive.

- Limited number of staff – apart from not having highly experienced staff, the organizations also complained of not having even enough staff to run their programs. As such, a lot of them depended on volunteers to help implement their programs.

In dealing with the lack of human and financial resources, high-performing organizations did some of four things:

- They looked inward to untapped resources in the organization.
- They looked inward to their board for assistance.
- They looked outward to their peers.
- They looked outward to funders and external partners.

Looked inward to untapped resources – Lack of funds made organizations use their staff instead of consultants to drive the capacity building process. One of the executive directors told me that using staff instead of external consultants was a very tough transition for them to make because they already had an organizational mindset that capacity building is done by consultants. However, he was glad they used their staff as internal consultants because it helped to develop the capacity and expertise of the staff in a way they had not experienced previously. Another organization that was a membership organization raised $40,000 for capacity building by reaching out to their members and volunteers and getting them more actively engaged in the organization. According to the executive director "that was a great achievement for us because it was the first time we were raising money from members and volunteers."

Looked inward to the board – Engaging the board was another way organizations dealt with the challenges of limited human and financial resources. Some organizations tapped into the technical expertise of their board members to build their capacity and mentor their staff. One of the executive directors said "The board supported the organization. They mentored the staff and the volunteers. Some even went down to the community to support and review the programs. These were the major factors for success." In some other organizations, they got their boards to be more involved in raising funds for the organization.

Looked outward to colleagues – Some of the organizations asked for help from other organizations in order to overcome the challenges in meeting their goals. Quite a number of organizations asked for help from bigger international non-governmental organizations in areas such as strategic planning, proposal writing, and external communication strategy, among others. Some NGOs in Ethiopia asked their NGO consortium to loan them staff for a specific period of time to help them work on specific capacity building projects--such as, fund raising and financial management.

Looked outward to funders and external partners – Some of the organizations set up fund raising units to drive fund raising for their capacity building and other projects. Some organizations sent the capacity assessment report and their capacity building plan to their current donors and asked for extra funds to implement their capacity building plan. Some of those requests were successful. One of the executive directors of the high-performing NGOs told me that it took some negotiation and some back and forth with the donors but that at the end they got money from their donors that was enough to implement their capacity building plan.

In summary, though goal setting was important for organizations to achieve change, persevering in the goals in the midst of challenges differentiated those who accomplished their goals from those who did not.

Chapter Summary

In organizations, setting goals is important in motivating people to increase productivity.

Importance of goal setting:

- Goals help to direct attention and effort to activities that are relevant to achieving the goal and away from irrelevant activities.
- Goals energize people for action. The higher the goal, the more the effort people put in.
- Goals encourage persistence. Having a goal makes people persist to accomplish it.
- Goals encourage innovation. Goals make people discover or use task relevant knowledge and strategies.
- Goals help individuals and teams to self-regulate and self-manage their performances.

Characteristics of motivating goals:

- Clear and specific
- Challenging
- Achievable
- Rewarding
- Simple

How to make goal setting effective in improving productivity:

- Public commitment to the goal
- Break up big goals into smaller goals
- Improve self-efficacy and capacity to attain goal
- Provide supportive feedback
- Build up enthusiasm for the goal
- Reduce goal conflicts

CHAPTER 5
USING THE ANTS' STRATEGY

"Teamwork is the secret that makes common people achieve uncommon results"

– Ifeanyi Onuoha

"No one can whistle a symphony. It takes a whole orchestra to play it."

– HE Luccock

I was fascinated to see the level of coordination among some ants as I watched them drag a piece of cookie. Some pulled the cookie while others pushed it to move it in the desired direction. None of the ants could move the cookie all alone and it took coordinated teamwork to get the job done. This same teamwork strategy that helps ants to achieve great results was one of the characteristics of the high-performing organizations in our study. While 75% of the high-performing NGOs in Nigeria reported using teamwork for their capacity building, only 23% of the low-performing NGOs reported teamwork. For a lot of the high-performing organizations, teamwork was already part of their organizational culture. Teamwork was seen not only as a step in accomplishing goals, but was also used in setting the goals and deciding the best way to accomplish them.

The high-performing organizations assigned the task of improving their organizational capacities to team(s) within their organizations. These teams were either specially created for the task (project teams) or they were existing teams in the organizations. The most effective teams were self-directed teams that had both management and non-management staff as their members. Traditionally, work teams are managed by supervisors who decide on what should be done, how it should be done, and who does what in a team. However, self-directed work teams are teams where team members are involved in making the decisions that supervisors traditionally make. Self-directed work teams have been shown to lead to improved productivity and quality and reduced cost in an organization. [1] In this chapter, I will outline scholarly findings on the advantages and disadvantages of teamwork in organizations, the things that a manager should consider while forming teams, and how to use brainstorming to improve team decision-making.

Advantages of teamwork

These are some of the advantages of teamwork:

Generation of more ideas - There is a greater amount of information, ideas, perspectives, skills, and experiences in a group than in a single individual. So, problems that require the use of knowledge are better handled by a group than by an individual. [2] If a group decision-making process is well managed, decisions taken in a group are richer than those taken as individuals.

Easier acceptance of decisions - When people are involved in deciding the solution to a problem, it is easier for them to take ownership of such decisions and be committed to their success. The acceptance of a decision in an organization might be more important than the quality of the decision. A bad decision that is well accepted is more likely to succeed than a great decision that lacks acceptance. [2]

Better understanding of decisions - Group decision-making leads to better understanding of the decisions. The team members do not need anyone to communicate the decision to them as they were part of the process. Being part of the decision-making process makes people understand how the decision was reached, the alternatives that were considered and rejected, and the considerations that went into the decision-making. [2] Such an understanding is deeper than the kind that will emerge if the decision were taken by the executive and communicated to the staff, no matter how detailed the communication might be. Thus, the challenge of insufficient communication will be reduced with group decision-making.

Setting higher goals - When people take group decisions it leads to setting and achieving higher goals compared to when decisions are taken and goals are assigned by a supervisor. [3] It is easier for a group to come to a decision to take a big risk than for individuals. So, group decision-making can lead to increased productivity.

More motivated staff - The support and reassurance of being members of a team makes people feel secure and provides an avenue for people to bond together and get to know each other better. It also makes people feel they are contributing to dealing with something important in the organization. The increased interpersonal relationships and sense of contributing meaningfully to the organization helps to motivate people to put in their best for the organization. [2,3]

Disadvantages of teamwork and how to deal with them

Working in teams has its disadvantages which managers should be aware of and take steps to prevent. The following are some of the disadvantages:

Individual dominance - Some individuals with strong opinions can dominate group decisions. People with such domineering personalities might make others agree with their opinions even when it is not the best for the team. [2] To deal with this, the group leader should make sure that everyone in the group gets a fair opportunity to air his or her views. Even when it seems everyone agrees with the views of an eloquent or domineering team member, the group leader should accept that view, but still press for a second option. This will encourage people to bring up alternative ideas which might end up being better than the earlier view.

Conflicts - Conflicts are bound to occur in groups and can either help or mar the group depending on how they are handled. Teams should take immediate steps to reduce conflicts that can have a negative effect on team performance – such as, personal attacks, dislike among group members, and racial disharmony (affective or relationship conflicts). However, there are some conflicts that are beneficial to teams which can be promoted. Moderate amounts of conflict relating to differences in ideas and opinions on how best to fulfill a task can actually be beneficial to groups (substantive or task conflicts). [4] High-performing groups have been found to be groups that have less of affective conflicts and more of task conflicts. [5]

The first step to deal with conflicts is to first diagnose the type of conflict and the root cause of the conflict. [4] Teams should have open discussions about conflicts and this will help them to understand the source of the conflicts, clarify misconceptions, and deal with the conflicts. Conflicts when well-handled lead to a more cohesive team and increased productivity.

Time requirement - Group meetings can be time-consuming and unproductive if members do not prepare ahead of time for meetings. To prevent this, group leaders should ensure that the agendas of meetings are distributed ahead of meeting time. Although it is important to be efficient with time management, group leaders should allow issues to be well discussed before reaching a decision on the issues. [2]

Role of the team leader

Team leaders play important roles in the success of the team. Some of these roles are as follows:

Focuses team on goal and influences expectation - The team leader has the task of communicating the vision and focusing the team on the goals they need to accomplish. [6] Team leaders should state and restate the purpose and importance of their teams' assignments. They should also state and restate their confidence in the skill and ability of their teams to achieve their goals.

Encourages team self-management - Team leaders in self-managing teams have important roles to play in the success of the teams. According to Manz et al. (1987) these roles include the following: [7]

1. Facilitating self-goal setting (encourage group to set their own performance goal)
2. Facilitating self-expectation (encourage group to have high expectations for group performance)
3. Facilitating self-criticism (encourage group to be critical of low group performance)
4. Facilitating self-reinforcement (encourage group to reward and reinforce high group performance)

5. Facilitating self-evaluation (encourage group to monitor and evaluate their progress)

Facilitates communication - The team leader facilitates communication in the team. [6,7] He or she ensures that everyone contributes during discussions and that no one is allowed to dominate the discussion. He or she also ensures that the discussion is on track and steers the discussion back if the team is veering off track. The team leader should also be a good listener and develop the skills of summarizing the options discussed in the group so that the group can arrive at a decision.

Facilitates conflict resolution - Conflicts are usual and natural for a team. The role of the leader is to quickly identify and facilitate the conflict resolution process. He or she makes room for open discussion of conflicts as soon as they are discovered. The team leader also takes responsibility for group failures and does not blame individual team members for group failures.

Things managers need to consider while forming teams

Team autonomy - One characteristic of high-performing teams in my study is that the teams had autonomy to decide on their work processes and who does what in the team. Autonomy in work teams is associated with employee satisfaction, enhanced worker attitudes and behavior, and improved overall organizational performance. [8] However, there are mixed findings on the impact of autonomy in the effectiveness of project teams (teams formed to deal with a specific project). One study in South Korea showed that autonomy was more effective when the project team had a large workload and the organization's work climate favored innovation. [8]

Team tasks should be assigned to teams - Managers should ensure that the tasks that are assigned to teams are the ones that require a team to handle. Assigning tasks that are narrow, which would be best handled by individuals, to a team will be a waste of organizational resources.

Diversity of team - As much as possible, the team should have people with different types of experiences, perspectives, and skill sets. This will help to ensure that the team has the resources (knowledge and skills) it needs to function effectively. A likely drawback of team diversity is that a high level of team diversity may inhibit social integration and team cohesion, but this level of diversity is unlikely in teams with members from the same organization.

Size of team - The size of the team depends on the type and complexity of the task to be carried out. Studies have shown a U-shaped relationship between the size of the team and its effectiveness. [1] Teams that are too small or too large may not be very efficient. Small teams may not have all the knowledge and skill sets in the group to effectively accomplish the task; while, large teams might be too large to effectively coordinate and get everyone actively involved.

Reward - Teams should be rewarded as a team. Managers should not reward employees individually for work done as a team. For instance, managers should not praise some individuals and leave out others for work that was performed as a team. Collective reward motivates teams to work harder as a team. [9] Managers should also ensure that the reward is aligned with the task.

Accountability - Team members should be accountable to the team and the team should be accountable to the organization. Teams, including self-directed work teams, should be made to give intermittent reports of their progress to the organization. This will provide an opportunity to give feedback to the team where needed.

Team brainstorming as a way of improving quality of team decisions

One way teams improve the quality of their decisions is through brainstorming. Brainstorming originated and was first used by Osborn who suggested brainstorming as a way of increasing the quantity and quality of ideas in group problem solving. [10,11] Brainstorming is the process where a group of individuals produces a wide range of ideas and creatively thinks through the ideas to combine and improve them until they agree on a solution to a problem. The assumption is that the greater the number of ideas produced, the greater the probability of getting an effective solution. [10] Osborn was of the opinion that while there are gains in working as a team, the effectiveness and creativity of team decisions are reduced due to the practice of prematurely evaluating ideas as they are generated. [12] He outlined four basic principles of brainstorming:

1. No criticism of ideas during the brainstorming period.
2. Express all ideas no matter how unconventional, bizarre, radical, or impracticable they may appear. The wider the range of ideas, the better.
3. Generate as many ideas as possible. The greater the number of ideas the greater the likelihood of getting the best solution.
4. Combine and improve one another's ideas.

The idea of brainstorming is to remove the inhibition, self-criticism, and fear of criticism from others that inhibit creative thinking in a team. It encourages the generation of as many ideas as possible in order to find the most effective team solution to a problem.

However, studies have shown that contrary to Osborn's assertion, group participation using brainstorming actually inhibits creative thinking. One of such studies was done and published by Taylor et al. in 1958. Taylor et al. asked subjects to brainstorm individually or as a group of four persons for 12 minutes. Thereafter, they compared the ideas generated by the real groups to that generated by nominal groups. Nominal groups were formed by randomly combining the result of four people who brainstormed individually. So the nominal group ideas represent the ideas that would have been generated if group interaction did not facilitate or inhibit generation of ideas. They found that the total number of ideas, the total number of unique ideas, and the quality of ideas produced through brainstorming by the real groups were substantially inferior to those from the nominal groups. [10] Several studies have suggested reasons for the difference in brainstorming productivity between real and nominal groups. Some of these reasons are as follows:

Production blocking – due to the fact that only one member speaks at a time, other members of the group will not verbalize their ideas as they come and may forget them. In addition, listening to the ideas of other group members may interfere with subject's own thinking. [11]

Evaluation apprehension – despite the brainstorming rules, individuals in a group may fear the negative evaluation of other group members even if the evaluation is not verbalized. [10,11]

Free riding – when people brainstorm in a group, individual productivity is not easily noticed and that might be a disincentive to contribute ideas. In addition, some individuals might hold back their contributions because they feel that their contributions in the group will not make much of a difference. [11]

Conformity – when people work in a group, they are more likely to pursue the same line of thoughts compared to the same number of individuals working alone. [10]

Enhancing group brainstorming

Several methods have been shown to reduce production blocking, evaluation apprehension, free riding, and conformity and to improve group brainstorming productivity. Some ways teams can enhance the effectiveness of their brainstorming are the following:

1. **Combination of group and individual brainstorming** – this involves brainstorming first as a group and then brainstorming individually. This has been shown to generate more ideas than brainstorming first individually before brainstorming as a group. [13]

2. **Individual brainwriting** – in individual brainwriting, each member of the team first brainstorms individually and writes down his or her ideas on a paper. Then each person reads out his or her ideas and the ideas are written down. The team then evaluates the ideas and combines or modifies them to reach a consensus. In this way, group inhibition in the production of ideas is eliminated. [13]

3. **Group brainwriting** – group brainwriting involves individual group members writing their ideas on a piece of paper and passing it on to the next group member, who reads the ideas, includes his or her own ideas and passes it to the next group member. Group brainwriting was shown to be more effective than individual brain writing in heterogeneous groups where members have differing knowledge of the brainstorming problem. [13]

4. Electronic brainstorming – in electronic brainstorming, each member of the group works independently on a computer and the ideas generated are displayed anonymously on a screen. Using this method, production blocking is eliminated and more ideas are generated. [13]

5. Nominal group technique (NGT) – in NGT, each team member individually brainstorms and writes down his or her ideas. Team members then share the ideas with the group in a round-robin fashion and the ideas are recorded. The ideas are then discussed for further understanding and clarification. At the end of the discussion, individual team members privately rank the ideas and the final choice is made based on the summation of the individual rankings. [12,14]

In conclusion, to improve productivity in organizations, managers should understand the importance of groups, whether formal or informal. Decisions taken by a group tend to be more valuable than decisions taken by an individual. [4] Hence management should not only encourage formation of groups in organizations, they should also help groups to succeed. One way to do this is to ensure that when appropriate, tasks are assigned to groups instead of individuals. In addition, the actions of managers should make employees understand that being an active member of a group is valued. Staff in a group should be appreciated and rewarded for being part of a successful group rather than for individual efforts.

Furthermore, managers can help groups succeed by teaching staff how to effectively handle conflicts in groups and how to effectively moderate group meetings. Management should as much as possible use the suggestions from groups/employees. However, if the suggestions from a group will not be used at the moment, management should appreciate the group for their effort and let them know that their suggestions are highly valued even if not implemented.

Chapter summary

Teamwork is another characteristic of high-performing organizations.

Advantages of teamwork:

- More ideas are generated
- Easier acceptance of decisions
- Better understanding of decisions
- Setting higher goals
- More motivated staff

Disadvantages of teamwork:

- Individual dominance
- Conflicts
- Time requirement

Things managers need to consider while forming teams:

- Team autonomy
- Team tasks should be assigned to teams
- Diversity of team
- Size of team
- Team reward
- Team accountability

Ways of enhancing group brainstorming:

- Combination of group and individual brainstorming
- Individual brainwriting
- Group brainwriting
- Electronic brainstorming
- Nominal group technique (NGT)

CHAPTER 6
SHOWING EACH OTHER THE WAY

"Tell me and I forget, teach me and I may remember, involve me and I learn."

— Benjamin Franklin

"In learning you will teach, and in teaching you will learn."

— Phil Collins

Peer mentoring was reported by 17% of the high-performing organizations and 0% of the low-performing organizations. Although it was 17% of the high-performing organizations that reported peer mentoring, these were the top tier change organizations that had instituted a learning culture in their organizations. Mentoring provides an opportunity for individuals in an organization to share knowledge and build the intellectual capacity of each other. Mentoring is when someone who has deep knowledge about an issue (mentor) teaches or guides another (mentee). [1]

There are different types of mentoring, including these:

- Traditional mentoring (senior employees mentor junior employees)
- Peer mentoring (mentoring involving peers)
- Co-mentoring (mentor and mentee learn from each other in a mutual, reciprocal relationship)
- "Mentoring up" or reverse mentoring (junior employees mentor senior employees)
- Team or group mentoring (informational sharing, social support, and coaching within a group)
- E-mentoring (mentoring through online software or email).

Mentoring has been associated with greater staff retention, productivity, career advancement, psychosocial well-being, induction to the organization, professionalism, and job satisfaction. Mentoring benefits both the mentor and the mentee. For the mentors, it gives them the self-satisfaction of seeing their mentees advance and succeed in their careers.[2] Mentors have also reported increased competence, increased confidence in their abilities, and increased esteem among their peers. [3]

For the mentees, mentoring plays two broad functions, a career enhancing function and a psychosocial function. As a career enhancer, mentoring provides an avenue to share technical and job-related information (information sharing), discuss career challenges, discuss plans and options (career strategizing), and get feedback on work done which is helpful for growth and improvement (job-related feedback). For its psychosocial function, mentoring provides an avenue for emotional support, personal feedback, and friendship. [4]

Peer mentoring

Peer mentoring is a learning relationship in which peers (employees at the same or similar level) learn from each other. [5] Peer mentoring plays a role in the socialization of new employees (acquiring the knowledge, attitude, and behaviors they need to function as effective members of the organization). [5] It provides opportunities for employees to learn from multiple peers with diverse experiences. It also provides an opportunity for non-hierarchical, personalized, goal-specific learning. [2] In addition, peer mentoring provides the opportunity for the mentee to be the mentor in different scenarios. Furthermore, it makes the junior employees not to be dependent on their supervisors or senior employees. [5] Peer mentoring can be between peers in the same organization or in separate organizations.

The non-hierarchical nature of peer mentoring makes communication, mutual support, and collaboration easier than in a traditional mentoring relationship. [4] Peer relationships appear to last longer than most of the other mentoring relationships and can provide continuity over the course of an employee's career. While traditional mentoring seems to be very important at the start of one's career, peer mentoring appears to be very important at every stage of one's career. Unlike traditional mentoring, peer mentoring is readily available to individuals in an organization because there are a greater number of people who can be peer mentors compared to those who can be traditional mentors. [4,5]

Table 1: Comparison of Traditional, One-on-One, and Group Peer Mentoring

	Traditional	1 – 1 peer mentoring	Group peer mentoring
Personal relationship	x	x	
Individualized	x	x	
Confidentiality and safe environment for mistakes	x	x	
Multiple levels of expertise and knowledge			x
Diverse perspectives			x
Teamwork and networking			x
Competition		x	x
Group projects			x
More demand on time	x	x	
Topics might be irrelevant to some people			x
Multi-directional learning		x	x

Peer mentoring could be one-on-one mentoring or group mentoring. One-on-one peer mentoring involves two peers who are learning from each other while group mentoring involves peers learning from each other in a group. Both forms have advantages and disadvantages and organizations need to decide the one that works best for them based on their resources and peculiarities.

Advantages of one-on-one peer mentoring

Some advantages of one-on-one peer mentoring are that it does the following:
- Provides individualized mentoring
- Provides relationship and psychosocial support
- Provides a confidential and safe environment for mistakes and learning
- Provides career-enhancing functions
- Provides opportunity for mutual learning between mentor and mentee

Disadvantages of one-on-one peer mentoring

These are some of the disadvantages of one-on-one peer mentoring:
- Perpetuation of wrong knowledge or work ethics – employees with incorrect technical information or work attitudes can pass it on to their peer mentees.
- Stifling of innovation and change – information and procedures already being used in the workplace are passed to others. This might prevent mentees from seeking new ways of solving problems.
- Mentors or mentees can be exploitative, self-serving, and only interested in advancing their careers – peer mentoring involves sharing information and knowledge that will be beneficial to each other. Some employees might only

be interested in what they can benefit from the relationship and not what they can contribute. [6]
- Overloading the efficient mentors (personally and professionally competent mentors) – peers might want to be mentored by the knowledgeable and efficient peers and this might lead to work overload for such mentors. [6]
- Competition and jealousy – mentors might feel threatened by the mentees professional growth. [6]
- Mentees can become overly dependent on mentors.

Advantages of group peer mentoring

The following are some advantages of group peer mentoring:
- Teamwork and a collaborative approach to learning [6]
- Multiple perspectives and experiences in the group
- Less time-consuming and more efficient use of resources [6]
- Addresses the challenges of one-on-one cross-sex peer mentoring (to be discussed later)[6]
- Provides career enhancing functions

Disadvantages of group peer mentoring

Some disadvantages of group peer mentoring are as follows:
- Less interpersonal relationship and psychosocial support
- Lack of individualized and customized learning
- Topics being learned might be irrelevant to some people in the group

One-on-one and group peer mentoring – Examples from the field

I will briefly discuss two high-performing organizations in our study that used peer mentoring. The first organization (nonprofit A) used group peer mentoring while the second (nonprofit B) used one-on-one peer mentoring.

Nonprofit A

Nonprofit A is a small nonprofit organization where staff play different roles at different times depending on the project they are working on. Nonprofit A set up a group peer mentoring program to improve staff learning. The peer mentoring occurs every week and different staff are assigned different topics to teach their peers based on their areas of specialty. Staff who had attended external training/workshops use the peer mentoring sessions to teach their peers new or innovative things they learned. The peer meeting time creates opportunity to learn new things or reinforce the things already learned. Staff are encouraged to research new and innovative ways of doing things and teach others. In addition, staff are encouraged to create an active learning environment using group discussions, demonstrations, and role plays. All staff receive prior information of the topics to be discussed and are encouraged to come prepared to contribute to the discussion.

Nonprofit B.

Nonprofit B engaged in task specific one-on-one peer mentoring. Staff are paired for specific projects based on their knowledge and skills in different areas. So, for instance, if the organization needs a logic model for a project, a staff who knows how to prepare a logic model is paired with another who does not and both of them will work on the task. In this way, the one with the knowledge teaches the other. The training is hands on and the mentee gets an opportunity to learn and practice. The beauty of this is that everyone is involved in teaching and learning. So the person who is a mentor today might be a mentee tomorrow depending on the task that is being carried out. In that way they built an organization where there is a lot of interpersonal interaction within the staff and a strong sense of community.

Formal and informal peer mentoring – What the literature says

Most mentoring relationships are informal and develop due to shared interests and values and job demands that require more than one person. Most informal mentoring involves not only discussing technical and job related issues, but also discussing personal interests, needs, and values. [7]

However, many organizations are formalizing the mentoring relationship by assigning mentors to mentees in order to reap the benefits of mentoring such as employee socialization, technical training, and personal and professional development. Formal mentoring relationships might not be as effective as the informal ones due to personality differences between the mentors and mentees and a lack of personal commitment of the mentors or mentees to the assigned mentorship relationship since it was not voluntarily entered into. [7]

Some other challenges to formal mentoring include time limitations; incompatible work schedules and physical distance; poor planning of the program; unsuccessful matching of mentors and mentees (professional expertise or personality mismatch or incompatibility based on race or gender); and lack of understanding about the mentoring relationship. [6-8]

Steps to set up successful formal mentoring programs

Certain characteristics of a formal mentoring program have been shown to improve its effectiveness. Managers should ensure that formal mentoring programs include the following characteristics:

Clearly defined mentoring goals – this helps the mentor and mentee know the purpose of the mentoring relationship and enables them to evaluate if the program has been successful. In programs where mentees chose their mentors, knowing the purpose of the mentoring relationship will also help them choose the right mentors. [7]

Voluntary participation – participation by both mentors and mentees should be voluntary. People who voluntarily decide to participate show greater motivation to participate and have greater satisfaction from the program than those who are forced to participate. [7]

Choice of mentor/mentee – As much as possible employees should be allowed to have a say in who they will mentor or who will mentor them. This leads to greater likelihood of compatibility and interpersonal similarity. [9] Similarities between mentor and mentee such as in backgrounds, interests, and workstyles increase the effectiveness of the mentoring relationship. [10] Participants taking part in deciding their mentor/mentee also makes the participants take ownership of the program and be more committed to its success. [11]

Training for both mentor and mentee – this helps both the mentor and mentee to understand the program, the importance, the participants' roles, the expectations for meetings and interactions between mentor and mentee, and the expected outcomes. Training helps to manage the expectation from the program and increases commitment to the success of the program. [11] Other topics that could be taught in the training include how to prepare for meeting; how to create an action plan; how to focus on and communicate key information, learning styles, and learning assessments; and how to formalize mentoring relationships. [5]

Support of top level management – formal mentoring programs need the support of top level management to succeed. The management should be able to approve a paid out-of-work time for the mentor and mentee to meet. Furthermore, management support in providing training for the mentors and mentees is critical to the success of the program.

Non-judgmental approach – providing a safe environment where people feel they can make mistakes and learn without being judged or disrespected is essential for a successful mentoring program.

Monitoring and evaluation – continuous monitoring is essential during the mentoring relationship in order to discover problems early enough and solve them. There is also need for a final evaluation of the program based on the goals the program set out to achieve.

Other things managers need to consider when setting up formal peer mentoring

Gender – Gender should be considered in matching mentors and mentees. As much as possible, people should play a part in deciding who they will mentor or who will mentor them. There are advantages and there are challenges associated with cross-sex mentoring relationships. Some of the advantages of cross-sex mentoring include the fact that female mentors have been reported to provide more career and psychosocial functions to their mentees compared to male mentors. [7,10,12] Additionally, mentees in a cross-sex mentoring relationship more effectively utilize the mentor compared to those in a same sex mentoring relationship. Male-male mentoring relationship was reported as less effectively utilized compared to female-female or cross-sex mentoring relationship. [7]

However, there are challenges associated with cross-sex mentoring relationships. First, some people might not be comfortable in a cross-sex mentoring relationship. Larwood (1978) found that in the workplace, men and women prefer interacting with people of the same sex. [13] Second, the relationship between the mentor and mentee in cross-sex mentoring may be perceived as sexual which might lead to workplace gossip; jealousy and resentment; and pressure on mentee or mentor (even from spouses) to end such a relationship. So, while mentors and mentees of the same sex might become friends and socialize within and outside the work environment, cross-sex mentors and mentees may be constrained from developing a similar level of friendship which might hamper the mentoring relationship. Third, abuses of cross-sex mentoring relationships in form of sexual or over-extended relationships have been reported. [6]

So, the bottom line is that as much as possible, employees should be given an opportunity to make an input on the gender of their mentor/mentee.

Frequency of meeting – Frequent communication should be encouraged between the mentor and mentee. Mentors who communicated more frequently with their mentees provided them more career and psychosocial support. [10] To ensure that meeting time is maximized, peer mentors should draw out a plan of what they will achieve during each meeting. In addition, organizations can help mentors and mentees maximize the relationship by requiring a minimum number of meetings between the mentor and mentee within a specified time period.

Duration of mentoring – Longer acquaintance between mentor and mentee leads to greater career and psychosocial support. [10] So mentoring relationships should be long enough to achieve their goals.

Physical proximity of mentor and mentee – Mentoring relationships provided more career and psychosocial functions when the offices of the mentor and mentee were close. [10] Managers should ensure that mentees have access to their mentors and that as much as possible there is geographical proximity.

Chapter summary

Mentoring provides an opportunity for individuals in an organization to share knowledge and build the intellectual capacity of each other.

Peer mentoring can be one-on-one mentoring or group mentoring.

Advantages of one-on-one peer mentoring:

- Individualized mentoring
- Personal relationship and psychosocial support
- Confidential and safe environment for mistakes and learning
- Career-enhancing functions
- Opportunity for mutual learning between mentor and mentee

Advantages of group peer mentoring:

- Teamwork and a collaborative approach to learning
- Multiple perspectives and experiences in the group
- Less time-consuming and more efficient use of resources
- Addresses the challenges of one-on-one cross-sex peer mentoring
- Provides career enhancing functions

How managers can make formal mentoring programs succeed:

- Clearly define mentoring goals
- Make participation voluntary
- Give employees a say in the choice of their mentor or mentee
- Provide training for both mentor and mentee
- Provide support of top level management
- Promote non-judgmental mentoring approach
- Provide monitoring and evaluation of mentoring program
- Ensure adequate mentoring meeting

CHAPTER 7
EMPLOYING THE POWER OF SYNERGY

"Our greatest strength lies in collaboration, not competition."

— Joseph Rain

"Alone we can do so little; together we can do so much"

— Helen Keller

The last characteristic of high-performing nonprofit organizations in our study was that they were engaged in different levels of collaboration with other organizations. Whereas 50% of the high-performing organizations reported they were involved in peer-to-peer collaboration, 15% of the low-performing organizations reported such collaboration. Guo et al. (2005) identified eight levels of collaboration between organizations which can be grouped into informal collaboration (information sharing, referral of clients, sharing of office spaces, and management service organization) and formal collaboration (joint program, parent subsidiary, joint venture, and merger). [1] Collaborations can also be horizontal (between organizations doing similar work) or vertical (organizations playing different roles) [2]

Collaborations, alliances, and social networks have been shown to help organizations improve their performance. This is more so in donative organizations (organizations that rely on donations) than for commercial organizations (organizations involved in commercial activities to raise funds). Collaborations and networks have been known to be more beneficial to young resource-constrained organizations as they help them get access to resources from more established organizations. [3] Young nonprofits in networks have been known to survive more than those who are working all alone.

Nonprofit collaboration – experience from the field

Social networks and collaborations played a critical role in the improvement of the nonprofit organizations we worked with. Most of the organizations belonged to umbrella nonprofit organizations. Some organizations had managers who made much better use of their networks than others whether they belonged to an umbrella organization or not. There were four levels of collaboration I saw in our study:

Collaboration between strong/reputable organizations – There were mutually beneficial collaborations between reputable organizations. During our study, there was a case of an organization that needed to upgrade its data management system and sought help from a partner organization which provided it with the information and support it needed. However, collaboration between competing organizations can lead to an organization wanting to get as much information as possible from a partner while divulging as little as possible in order to gain a competitive advantage. This notwithstanding, forming alliances with competitors has its own advantages, one of which is that shared experiences, skills, and resources can be very helpful.

Collaboration between weak and strong organizations - This was the most common type of collaboration I saw between organizations in our study. The less reputable organizations got information or skills from the stronger, more reputable organizations. While most of the more reputable organizations were open to helping the less reputable ones, we had an instance where a reputable organization refused to share information with a less reputable organization unless the weaker organization paid some money in exchange. There were also occasions where staff from smaller organizations who had been involved in collaborations with bigger organizations joined the bigger organizations after they had gained skills and built relationships with the bigger organizations.

I also noticed that collaboration does not only help smaller organizations build their capabilities, it also affects how third parties view their capabilities. Associating with organizations that were reputable was also helpful because donors and other stakeholders who did not know the small organizations judged them by the reputation of their networks and collaborators. I call this imputed reputation.

Collaboration between weak and weak organizations - This was also commonly seen. Managers who needed help usually went first to organizations they already had a relationship with which were usually organizations that looked more like them. When they did not get the information or resources they needed, then they went to other organizations. Collaborations between smaller organizations helped those organizations to learn things they might not have learned from bigger organizations. These smaller organizations have similar challenges, and have learned to innovate because they do not have as much resources as the bigger organizations.

Collaboration between weak organizations and umbrella associations - The umbrella associations played a great role in helping organizations, especially the weaker ones. They shared information, provided training to organizations in the association, and provided opportunities for referrals and sharing of resources. They also got big grants which they sub-granted to the smaller organizations. In addition, they occasionally sent staff on loan to weak organizations to help them in specific areas such as proposal development, setting up a financial management system, etc.

Making the best of the collaboration network – What worked

The importance of networks and collaborations has been noted in previous studies; however, the challenge is in how to get organizations to maximize the resources in their networks. From my experience, the following steps will help organizations utilize membership of an umbrella association or alliance:

Being an active member of the network – In our study, being a member of an umbrella organization was very helpful especially for the smaller organizations. However, getting the maximum benefit from such groups requires commitment and active participation as a member. This commitment might include attending meetings, conferences, and social events; serving in committees of the association; and providing support to other organizations. Being an active member makes it easier for organizations to build the type of relationships and trust that will lead to other organizations sharing resources and information with them. Thus, it makes sense to join a network only when the profit from the network is greater than the investment needed to keep relationships in the network. So, it is not just joining an alliance or umbrella association that matters, the manager must be ready to invest time and resources to get the best out of the alliance.

Building friendship over time – We found that it is not just belonging to a social network that is important, but building relationships and friendships in the network. Building relationships has a multiplier effect because one's friends can link one up with the other's friends. Organizations sometimes help other organizations with information, capital, clients, facilities, and other material resources because of the relationships that have been built over time. Information diffuses unevenly in a network [10] and it is easier for organizations to work better with organizations that they have built up trust with over the years. Giving and receiving of favors is usually reciprocal and so it takes time to build up these relationships.

Asking for help when needed – Another way through which resources and information flow is by simply asking. Although it is easier to ask when there is a relationship, asking even when there is no relationship also works. We saw in our study that organizations that asked for help profited more from the consortium than those that did not. However, there were organizations that asked and did not receive the help they needed and stopped at that point, while there were others that persevered and sought assistance from different sources until they got what they wanted. So, in asking, organizations should be prepared to persevere until they get the information or resources they need.

Importance of nonprofit collaboration – what the literature says

Collaboration of nonprofit organizations has several advantages:

1. Improvement in status, reputation, and credibility of nonprofits – when less known organizations in the community collaborate with other well-known and reputable organizations, it gives

the less known organizations some credibility. This is very important with donative organizations (organizations that primarily rely on donations) because a lot of people and foundations make donations to organizations based on their status, reputation, and credibility. Similarly, people are more willing to volunteer in an organization that is reputable. In addition, donative nonprofits that rely heavily on donations and volunteers grow faster if they have good reputations and inter-organizational networks. [4]

2. Resource sharing between organizations – Nonprofits can share office space, staff, volunteers, capital, technology, and other material resources in order to achieve their mission. This form of collaboration can lead to growth, technology spillover, and innovation. [4-6]

3. Information (technical or environmental) sharing between organizations – one of the important roles of nonprofit collaboration is that it helps to speed up diffusion of both old and new information. This diffusion of information, strategies, and methods will be amplified if the organizations are similar in some ways. [4-6]

4. Joint projects – nonprofits can write grants and implement projects together. They can also pool their resources with other organizations to provide services. Additionally, they can collaborate to purchase goods and services in bulk at a lower price. [6]

5. Referrals among nonprofits – Referral of clients is another benefit of inter-organizational collaboration. In a survey of non-profits in rural Illinois and Mississippi, referral of clients and sharing of information were the commonest types of collaboration found among nonprofits. [4,6]

6. Increased survival of organizations – survival is very important for new organizations. New organizations usually have limited resources, lack stable relationships with important external stakeholders, and lack the reliability and legitimacy that older, more established organizations enjoy. Collaborations help them with the resources, relationships, and legitimacy they need to function effectively. [3-5,7]

7. Increased political influence – collaboration helps nonprofits to make important political connections that increase their influence. It also increases the visibility of the organization in the community. [4,6]

8. Improved performance of organizations – the combination of the various advantages of collaboration leads to improved performance of nonprofits. [4] Collaboration was reported as an effective way of delivering quality services to clients in rural Illinois and Mississippi. [6]

Disadvantages of nonprofit collaboration

There are disadvantages that can arise from collaboration of which nonprofit organizations should be aware. Here are some possible disadvantages:

1. The benefits might not offset the cost of maintaining and managing inter-organizational relationships. [4] There is a cost that comes with building and maintaining collaborative relationships. Collaboration can take significant amounts of staff time and organizational resources. [6] So, if an organization is in a collaboration where it is not gaining much in terms of shared information, resources, referrals, reputation, among others then the cost of keeping that collaboration might be more than the benefits.

2. Weakened or compromised organizational autonomy and boundaries – organizations involved in joint ventures can lose their autonomy and their control of certain decisions and processes. [4] Organizations might have to sacrifice their individual interests for the group interest for the collaboration to be effective.

3. Smaller organizations losing their staff to bigger ones in the network – smaller organizations, who usually pay less competitive salaries, might lose their experienced staff to bigger organizations in a collaboration. [4]

4. Intra-alliance rivalry and jealousy – there could be rivalry and competition between organizations in an alliance or collaboration. [3]

5. Exploitative relationship – bigger and stronger organizations might exploit smaller and weaker ones who have less bargaining power in a collaboration such as a joint venture. [3]

Building blocks of nonprofit collaboration

There are things that are necessary for an effective collaboration. They include the following:

1. Trust and reciprocity – a lot of the informal networks are built on trust and reciprocity rather than formal contracts. [5] Organizations will be willing and open to sharing information when they feel that partner organizations are also willing and open to sharing information. Trust also builds up when organizations know that partners will be honest, fulfill their commitments, and not take advantage of others. [8]

2. Mutual benefits – it is important that there are mutual benefits for organizations in a collaboration; if not, the collaboration might not be sustainable. The benefits can be tangible or intangible – such as joy in mentoring a smaller organization.

3. Similarity – networks and collaborations are easier to form if the organizations have similar status and power. [5] Atouba et al. (2015) reported that international non-governmental organizations are more likely to collaborate when they have the same status (legitimacy, recognition, or esteem); when they have closer founding dates; when they have common funding partners; and when they are headquartered in the same geographic region.[9] Similarity in status and power makes it easier for organizations to reciprocate the gestures they extend to each other and this could make for a strong and mutually beneficial collaboration. [5]

4. Diversity of alliance – though it is easier to form collaborations with similar organizations, organizations should deliberately ensure that they also collaborate with diverse organizations. Just increasing an organization's number of alliances is not as helpful as ensuring that alliances are with organizations that have diverse capabilities and pools of information.

5. Governance – the organizations in a collaboration or alliance need to decide on how they will make decisions that jointly affect them. They also need to decide how they will resolve conflicts and what the consequences of not following through with joint decisions will be. [8]

6. Administration – roles, responsibilities, and monitoring mechanisms have to be clarified in joint ventures and partnerships. [8]

Chapter summary

Collaborations, alliances, and social networks have been shown to help organizations improve their performances.

Advantages of nonprofit collaboration:

- Improves the status, reputation, and credibility of non-profits
- Leads to resource sharing between organizations
- Leads to information sharing between organizations
- Leads to joint projects
- Engenders client referrals among nonprofits
- Increases survival of organizations
- Increases political influence of organizations
- Improves performance of organizations

Disadvantages of nonprofit collaboration:

- Benefits might not offset the cost of maintaining and managing inter-organizational relationships.
- Can weaken or compromise organizational autonomy and boundaries.
- Can lead to smaller organizations losing their staff to bigger ones in the network.
- Can lead to intra-alliance rivalry and jealousy.
- Can lead to an exploitative relationship.

How to make the best of a collaborative network:

- Become an active member of the network.
- Build friendships over time.
- Ask for favors when you need them.

In final summation, from my experience working with nonprofit organizations, organizations that create the right atmosphere for change, have motivated staff, are goal oriented, work as a team, engage in peer mentoring, and collaborate with other organizations outperform those that do not.

REFERENCES

Chapter 2 - Preparing the nest for the golden egg

1. Johnson G. Managing strategic change—strategy, culture and action. Long range planning. 1992 Feb 29;25(1):28-36.

2. Ford JD, Ford LW. The role of conversations in producing intentional change in organizations. Academy of Management Review. 1995 Jul 1;20(3):541-70.

3. Ashkenas R, Jick T. From dialogue to action in GE work-out: Developmental learning in a change process. In W. Pasmore, & R. Woodman (Eds.), Research in organizational change and development, vol. 6: 267-287. Greenwich, CT: JAI Press.

4. Beer M, Eisenstat R, Spector B. Why change programs don't produce change. Harvard Business Review. 1990; 68(6): 158-166.

5. Scherr, A. 1989. Managing for breakthroughs in productivity. Human Resource Management, 28: 403-424

Quotes at the beginning of each chapter were from Goodreads. http://www.goodreads.com/quotes

Chapter 3 - Getting the staff in high spirits

1. Ryan RM, Deci EL. Intrinsic and extrinsic motivations: Classic definitions and new directions. Contemporary educational psychology. 2000 Jan 31;25(1):54-67.

2. Gagné M, Deci EL. Self-determination theory and work motivation. Journal of Organizational behavior. 2005 Jun 1;26(4):331-62.

3. Saari LM, Judge TA. Employee attitudes and job satisfaction. Human resource management. 2004 Dec 1;43(4):395-407.

4. Maslow AH. A theory of human motivation. Psychological review. 1943 Jul;50(4):370.

5. Herzberg F. One more time: How do you motivate employees. New York: The Leader Manager. 1986 Feb 18:433-48.

6. Wagner JA. Participation's effects on performance and satisfaction: A reconsideration of research evidence. Academy of management Review. 1994 Apr 1;19(2):312-30.

7. Kim S. Participative management and job satisfaction: Lessons for management leadership. Public administration review. 2002 Jan 1;62(2):231-41.

8. Bhatti KK, Qureshi TM. Impact of employee participation on job satisfaction, employee commitment and employee productivity. International Review of Business Research Papers. 2007 Jun;3(2):54-68.

9. Vroom, V. H. (1964). Work and motivation. In: Lindner JR. Understanding employee motivation. Journal of extension. 1998 Jun;36(3):1-8.

10. Lindner JR. Understanding employee motivation. Journal of extension. 1998 Jun;36(3):1-8.

11. Adams JS. Inequity in social exchange. Advances in experimental social psychology. 1965 Dec 31;2:267-99.

12. Oluwafemi OJ. Predictors of turnover intention among employees in Nigeria's oil industry. Organ Mark Emerg Econ. 2013; 4(98), 42-63.

13. Skinner BF. Science and human behavior. Simon and Schuster; 1953.

Chapter 4 - They took steps toward turning the invisible into the visible

1. Locke EA, Latham GP. Building a practically useful theory of goal setting and task motivation: A 35-year odyssey. American psychologist. 2002 Sep;57(9):705.

2. Locke EA, Shaw KN, Saari LM, Latham GP. Goal setting and task performance: 1969–1980. Psychological bulletin. 1981 Jul;90(1):125.

3. Latham GP, Locke EA. Goal setting – A motivational technique that works. In: Natemeyer WE, Hersey P. Classics of organizational behavior. Waveland Press, Inc. 2011.

4. Wood RE, Locke EA. Goal setting and strategy effects on complex tasks. In: Drach-Zahavy A, Erez M. Challenge versus threat effects on the goal–performance relationship. Organizational Behavior and Human Decision Processes. 2002 Jul 31;88(2):667-82.

5. Drach-Zahavy A, Erez M. Challenge versus threat effects on the goal–performance relationship. Organizational Behavior and Human Decision Processes. 2002 Jul 31;88(2):667-82.

6. Locke EA, Latham GP. New directions in goal-setting theory. Current directions in psychological science. 2006 Oct 1;15(5):265-8.

Chapter 5 – Using the ants' strategy

1. Cohen SG, Bailey DE. What makes teams work: Group effectiveness research from the shop floor to the executive suite. Journal of management. 1997 Jun 1;23(3):239-90.

2. Maier NR. Assets and liabilities in group problem solving: the need for an integrative function. Psychological review. 1967 Jul;74(4):239.

3. Latham GP, Locke EA. Goal setting—A motivational technique that works. Organizational Dynamics. 1979 Sep 1;8(2):68-80.

4. Afzalur Rahim M. Toward a theory of managing organizational conflict. International journal of conflict management. 2002 Mar 1;13(3):206-35.

5. Jehn KA, Mannix EA. The dynamic nature of conflict: A longitudinal study of intragroup conflict and group performance. Academy of management journal. 2001 Apr 1;44(2):238-51.

6. Bachiochi PD, Rogelberg SG, O'Connor MS, Elder AE. The qualities of an effective team leader. Organization Development Journal. 2000 Apr 1;18(1):11.

7. Manz CC, Sims Jr HP. Leading workers to lead themselves: The external leadership of self-managing work teams. Administrative Science Quarterly. 1987 Mar 1:106-29.

8. Kim Y, Lee B. R&D project team climate and team performance in Korea: A multidimensional approach. R&D Management. 1995 Apr 1;25(2):179-96.

9. Wageman R. Interdependence and group effectiveness. Administrative science quarterly. 1995 Mar 1:145-80.

10. Taylor DW, Berry PC, Block CH. Does group participation when using brainstorming facilitate or inhibit creative thinking?. Administrative Science Quarterly. 1958 Jun 1:23-47.

11. Diehl M, Stroebe W. Productivity loss in brainstorming groups: Toward the solution of a riddle. Journal of personality and social psychology. 1987 Sep;53(3):497.

12. Meredith JR, Shafer SM. Operations management for MBAs. Fifth edition. Wiley & Sons. 2013

13. Brown VR, Paulus PB. Making group brainstorming more effective: Recommendations from an associative memory perspective. Current Directions in Psychological Science. 2002 Dec 1;11(6):208-12.

14. Deip P, Thesen A, Motiwalla J, Seshardi N. Systems tools for project planning. Bloomington, Indiana: International Development Institute. 1977

Chapter 6 - Showing each other the way

1. Swap W, Leonard D, Mimi Shields LA. Using mentoring and storytelling to transfer knowledge in the workplace. Journal of management information systems. 2001 May 31;18(1):95-114.

2. Mavrinac MA. Transformational leadership: Peer mentoring as a values-based learning process. portal: Libraries and the Academy. 2005;5(3):391-404.

3. Allen TD, Russell JE, Maetzke SB. Formal peer mentoring factors related to proteges' satisfaction and willingness to mentor others. Group & Organization Management. 1997 Dec 1;22(4):488-507.

4. Kram KE, Isabella LA. Mentoring alternatives: The role of peer relationships in career development. Academy of management Journal. 1985 Mar 1;28(1):110-32.

11. Bryant SE. The impact of peer mentoring on organizational knowledge creation and sharing an empirical study in a software firm. Group & Organization Management. 2005 Jun 1;30(3):319-38.

5. Long J. The dark side of mentoring. The Australian Educational Researcher. 1997 Aug 1;24(2):115-33.

6. Noe RA. An investigation of the determinants of successful assigned mentoring relationships. Personnel psychology. 1988 Sep 1;41(3):457-79.

7. Ehrich LC, Hansford B, Tennent L. Formal mentoring programs in education and other professions: A review of the literature. Educational administration quarterly. 2004 Oct 1;40(4):518-40.

8. Scott ME. (1992). Designing effect mentoring programs: Historical perspectives and current issues. In: Allen TD, Eby LT, Lentz E. The relationship between formal mentoring program characteristics and perceived program effectiveness. Personnel Psychology. 2006 Mar 1;59(1):125-53.

9. Burke RJ, McKeen CA, McKenna C. Correlates of mentoring in organizations: The mentor's perspective. Psychological Reports. 1993 Jun 1;72(3):883-96.

10. Allen TD, Eby LT, Lentz E. The relationship between formal mentoring program characteristics and perceived program effectiveness. Personnel Psychology. 2006 Mar 1;59(1):125-53.

12. Burke RJ. (1984) Mentors in organizations. *Group and Organization Studies,* 9, 253-272.

13. Larwood, L., & Blackmore, J. (1978) Sex discrimination in manager selection: Testing predictions of the vertical dyad linkage model. In: Noe RA. Women and mentoring: A review and research agenda. Academy of management review. 1988 Jan 1;13(1):65-78.

Chapter 7 - Employing the power of synergy

1. Guo C, Acar M. Understanding collaboration among nonprofit organizations: Combining resource dependency, institutional, and network perspectives. Nonprofit and Voluntary Sector Quarterly. 2005 Sep 1;34(3):340-61.

2. Inkpen AC, Tsang EW. Social capital, networks, and knowledge transfer. Academy of management review. 2005 Jan 1;30(1):146-65.

3. Baum JA, Calabrese T, Silverman BS. Don't go it alone: Alliance network composition and startups' performance in Canadian biotechnology. Strategic management journal. 2000 Mar 1;21(3):267-94.

4. Galaskiewicz J, Bielefeld W, Dowell M. Networks and organizational growth: A study of community based nonprofits. Administrative Science Quarterly. 2006 Sep 1;51(3):337-80.

5. Brass DJ, Galaskiewicz J, Greve HR, Tsai W. Taking stock of networks and organizations: A multilevel perspective. Academy of management journal. 2004 Dec 1;47(6):795-817.

6. Snavely K, Tracy MB. Collaboration among rural nonprofit organizations. Nonprofit Management and Leadership. 2000 Dec 1;11(2):145-65.

7. Stinchcombe, A. L. (1965). 'Social structure and organizations'. In Baum JA, Calabrese T, Silverman BS. Don't go it alone: Alliance network composition and startups' performance in Canadian biotechnology. Strategic management journal. 2000 Mar 1;21(3):267-94.

8. Thomson AM, Perry JL. Collaboration processes: Inside the black box. Public administration review. 2006 Dec 1;66(s1):20-32.

9. Atouba YC, Shumate M. International Nonprofit Collaboration Examining the Role of Homophily. Nonprofit and Voluntary Sector Quarterly. 2015 Jun 1;44(3):587-608.

10. Stuart TE. Network positions and propensities to collaborate: An investigation of strategic alliance formation in a high-technology industry. Administrative science quarterly. 1998 Sep 1:668-98.

www.ingramcontent.com/pod-product-compliance
Lightning Source LLC
Chambersburg PA
CBHW051721170526
45167CB00002B/753